Tools for continuing professional development

Note

Healthcare practice and knowledge are constantly changing and developing as new research and treatments, changes in procedures, drugs and equipment become available.

The author and publishers have, as far as is possible, taken care to confirm that the information complies with the latest standards of practice and legislation.

Tools for continuing professional development

2nd Edition

edited by

Chia Swee Hong and Deborah Harrison

QUAY
BOOKS
A division of MA Healthcare Ltd

Quay Books Division, MA Healthcare Ltd, St Jude's Church, Dulwich Road, London
SE24 0PB

British Library Cataloguing-in-Publication Data
A catalogue record is available for this book

© MA Healthcare Limited 2012

ISBN-10: 1-85642-424-3
ISBN-13: 978-1-85642-424-0

Edited by Jessica Anderson

Cover design by Claire Majury, Fonthill Creative

Publishing Manager: Andy Escott

Printed by Mimeo, Huntingdon, Cambridgeshire

Contents

Contents

Foreword to the 2nd Edition

Health professionals have a duty to keep up to date with skills and knowledge in order to ensure best practice for patient care. Continuing professional development (CPD) is an integral part of maintaining one's registration in today's regulated healthcare setting. Maintaining and recording our CPD should take place not just for the benefit of regulatory bodies but also to improve and develop as a responsible healthcare professional. All levels of healthcare professional should engage in CPD and students who are training to become registered healthcare professionals also need to be encouraged to develop and record their professional development and to establish CPD as an integral aspect of their practice.

Few might argue against keeping up to date with their professional skills and knowledge. However, being able to formalise that activity, being able to show evidence for the activity, and produce an ongoing record is where the difficulty may arise for many. In highly pressured, busy and demanding lives, CPD activities can be pushed to one side for 'later', or activities may be carried out yet not recorded. However, there are ways to facilitate these activities and this encouraging and positive book not only shows possible routes to carrying out CPD but also provides guidance on ways in which the recording can be made easier.

CPD must support our needs and objectives as healthcare professionals as we work in the ever-changing demands of today's healthcare. We need to consider CPD as an integral part of our working lives, as a process that assists us to learn the knowledge and skills that will support us in delivering the best care and treatment that we can. As we endeavour to meet the challenges in our working lives, well-planned CPD activity can help us become more confident and productive for our patients and for ourselves, and we need to then record that activity for our employers and our professional and regulatory bodies.

CPD requires us to take time out to consider our needs, to plan activities in order to meet those needs and then to record the activities and their outcomes. Within this book, chapters provide signposts to readily attainable ways of carrying out CPD alongside everyday activity, such as using broadcast media through active engagement with intelligent and relevant factual television and radio programmes; using personal reflection in professional development; clarifying what reflection is and why one should do it; using critical incidents as events around which one can pivot reflective practice; journal clubs; peer observation within professional practice and so forth. Further chapters focus on modes of recording the activities: portfolios as valuable aids to collect and collate evidence regarding CPD; learning contracts in practice to aid prioritisation of CPD amongst all of the other daily demands of work; using SWOT analysis not only as a useful CPD activity but also as evidence of personal reflection on one's professional development.

The first edition of *Tools for continuing professional development* was well received across many professions and disciplines. I am delighted to see this second edition, which brings not just updated but also more diverse sources of information and evidence. This book provides a valuable resource for healthcare professionals to help them to identify how they, as individuals, can and should meet their continuing professional development requirements.

Professor Jacqueline Collier
November 2011

Preface to the 2nd Edition

The first edition of *Tools for Continuing Professional Development* came about as a result of a conference held at the University of East Anglia in 1997. The conference proceedings were published in the *International Journal of Therapy and Rehabilitation* and those articles formed the basis of the first edition. It has proved a useful little volume for students and qualified staff. It was published, however, in 2004 at a time when the legislation that governed professional regulation had changed and we acknowledged that everything was shifting, from the wider health and social care context right down to the terminology being used. One thing that we can state with certainty is; constant change is the one element of our working life that has remained the same.

This new edition still has at its core some of the original chapters. The tools used to facilitate and record continuing professional development (CPD) have stood the test of time and they remain useful. These chapters have been refreshed with new evidence where it is available and they incorporate current terminology. There are also new chapters which capture the increased sophistication of the processes used to facilitate CPD and they reflect the complex working environments that healthcare practitioners negotiate in the 21st century. The book covers tools that provide a method of facilitating professional development and a means of recording it. It also has a focus on process and covers the how and the why of CPD.

This edition has contributions from a wider range of AHPs than the first and many are written by an interprofessional team. The authors are primarily from the UK with a few international contributions. The chapters, which can stand alone, reflect a wide variety of different styles of writing which is indicative of the diverse authorship of this second edition. It also indicates the broad range of possible routes into engaging with CPD and readers will find both familiar tools and some innovative approaches in the chapters of the book

As with the first edition, this one is primarily written for students as well registered allied health professionals (AHPs) who are regulated by the Health Professions Council (HPC). Many of the methods and processes will have a wider application and will be useful for all healthcare professionals. There are two key drivers making engagement with CPD an essential activity and not a luxury.

The first is, of course, the HPC audit of CPD, and any professional registered with the HPC can be selected. The last chapter gives a first-hand account of this experience. The second driver is the current health and social care context where CPD might seem like a luxury, but actually it becomes more essential to ensure that the highest quality, evidence-based healthcare is provided.

Chia Swee Hong and Deborah Harrison
November 2011

List of contributors

Julie Collier is Business Development Manager, Health, University of East Anglia

Mick Collins is Lecturer in Occupational Therapy, University of East Anglia

Deborah Davys is Lecturer in Occupational therapy, University of Salford

Jo Geere is Lecturer in Physiotherapy, University of East Anglia

Anne Guyon is Lecturer in Speech and Language Therapy, University of East Anglia

Deborah Harrison is Lecturer in Occupational Therapy, University of East Anglia

Chia Swee Hong is Lecturer in Occupational Therapy, University of East Anglia

Eve Hutton is Senior Lecturer, Research Centre for Children, Families and Communities, Canterbury Christ Church University

Vivienne Jones is Senior Lecturer in Occupational Therapy, University of Salford

Jon Larner is Undergraduate Course Director for Physiotherapy, University of East Anglia

Rosemarie Mason is Lecturer in Occupational Therapy, University of East Anglia

Margaret McArthur is MSc Pre-registration Occupational Therapy Programme Director, University of East Anglia

Kevin McNamara is Lecturer in Pharmacy Practice, Faculty of Pharmacy and Pharmaceutical Sciences, Centre for Medicine Use and Safety, Monash University, Victoria, Australia and Research Fellow in Rural Pharmacy, Greater Green Triangle University Department of Rural Health, Flinders University and Deakin University, Victoria, Australia

Ann Moore is Professor of Physiotherapy and Director of the Clinical Research Centre for Health Professions at the School of Health Professions, University of Brighton

Emma Payne is Occupational Therapist at Derbyshire Royal Infirmary

Adrian Schoo is Professor of Physiotherapy and Head of Clinical Education, School of Medicine, Faculty of Health Sciences, Flinders University and Honorary staff member of the Greater Green Triangle University Department of Rural Health, Repatriation General Hospital, Adelaide, South Africa

Toby O Smith is Lecturer in Physiotherapy, University of East Anglia

Nicola Spalding is Senior Lecturer in Occupational Therapy, University of East Anglia

Karen Stagnitti is Associate Professor, Occupational Science and Therapy, Faculty of Health, School of Health and Social Development, Deakin University, Geelong, Australia

Richard Stephenson is Pro Vice-Chancellor and Dean, Faculty of Health, Education and Society, University of Plymouth

Jennie Vitkovitch is Lecturer in Speech and Language Therapy, University of East Anglia

Martin Watson is Senior Lecturer in Physiotherapy, University of East Anglia

Catherine Wells is Senior Lecturer in Occupational Therapy, University of East Anglia

Acknowledgements

We would like to thank our colleagues and students who have shared inspiring reflective accounts with us. We would particularly like to thank Thu Nguyen, Andy Escott and Jessica Anderson at Quay Books for their invaluable editorial support, and acknowledge the contributions from the following students: Emily Sturman, Speech and Language Therapy student, Holly Rous, pre-registration MSc Occupational Therapy student and James Carn, Physiotherapy student and Ryckie G Wade, Medical Student who did an online review of the 1st edition and made the following remarks:

Very good for those studying CPD modules ....Very succinct, no waffle, just to the point .... Hope a 2nd edition arrives soon.

Chapter 1

The place of portfolios within CPD

Introduction

Rosemarie Mason

The generation and upkeep of a portfolio has become increasingly important for medical, nursing and allied health professionals and, in many cases, is now compulsory. Portfolios have become part of the process of clinical governance and are often used to provide evidence of a commitment to continued learning. The concept of 'clinical governance' was first outlined in *A first class service: Quality in the new NHS* (Department of Health, 1998). It is facilitated by mandates for patient and public involvement in healthcare, audit, staff education and training, clinical effectiveness and risk management. The aim is to strengthen systems of professional self-regulation, which run parallel to managerial systems of quality control (Foster and Wilding, 2000).

The quality of work within the NHS is now stringently monitored by outside agencies. For example, while the principle of lifelong learning has been applied to professions throughout history, it is now something for which healthcare practitioners are accountable (Department of Health, 1999). The Government's White Paper, *Trust, assurance and safety* (Department of Health, 2007) aims to ensure that all statutorily-regulated health professions have arrangements in place for the revalidation of professional registration, through which they can periodically demonstrate their continued fitness to practise (Department of Health, 2007). This co-exists with the arrangement whereby every two years allied health professionals have to sign a professional declaration that they continue to meet the Health Professions Council's standards of proficiency for the safe and effective practice of their profession and that they continue to meet the standards for continuing professional development (Health Professions Council, 2010). Doctors and nurses have similar arrangements in place (General Medical Council, 2010; and Nursing and Midwifery Council, 2010).

The use of portfolios to support these arrangements is increasingly widespread and in most cases mandatory for continued registration (Swallow *et al*, 2006; Tochel *et al*, 2009; Health Professions Council, 2010; General Medical Council, 2010). This chapter will briefly outline the role of one regulatory body, the Health Professions Council and then go on to explore the fundamental characteristics of portfolios and their purpose.

The Health Professions Council

Since 2005 all health professionals registered with the Health Professions Council (HPC) must undertake continuing professional development (CPD) in order to stay registered. Fifteen professions are currently regulated by the HPC, which are:

- Art therapists
- Biomedical scientists
- Chiropodists/podiatrists
- Clinical scientists
- Dietitians
- Hearing aid dispensers
- Occupational therapists
- Operating department practitioners
- Orthoptists
- Paramedics
- Physiotherapists
- Practitioner psychologists
- Prosthetists/orthotists
- Radiographers
- Speech and language therapists.

The HPC defines CPD as:

A range of learning activities through which health professionals maintain and develop throughout their career to ensure that they retain their capacity to practice safely, effectively and legally within their evolving scope of practice.
(Health Professions Council, 2010)

There is an expectation that registrants will undertake CPD activity and record it in a portfolio in order to demonstrate that they have met the standards set by the HPC. Registrants must:

- Maintain a continuous, up-to-date and accurate record of their CPD activities
- Demonstrate that their CPD activities are a mixture of learning activities relevant to current or future practice
- Seek to ensure that their CPD has contributed to the quality of their practice and service delivery

- Seek to ensure that their CPD benefits the service user
- Upon request, present a written profile explaining how they have met the standards for CPD.
(Health Professions Council, 2010)

This is policed by the HPC asking a random sample of registrants to provide a CPD profile with evidence of how they have met these standards each time a profession renews its registration. A professional development portfolio is usually used as the basis on which to generate a CPD profile.

What is a portfolio?

A portfolio has been described as:

- A personal and complete record of [allied health professionals'] CPD activity (Health Professions Council, 2010)
- A purposeful collection of [nurses'] tangible and intangible skills (Twaddle and Johnson, 2007)
- A dossier of evidence collected over time that demonstrates a [doctor's] education and practice achievements (Wilkinson *et al*, 2002).

At the most basic level, portfolios are simply collections of evidence that learning activities have taken place, with the purpose of demonstrating the continuing acquisition of skills, knowledge, attitudes, understanding and achievement (Simpson and Courtney, 2002; Swallow *et al*, 2006). Other purposes reported in the literature include: the assessment of competence (Wilkinson *et al*, 2002; Endacott *et al*, 2004), development of reflective practice (Glaze, 2002), to link theory with practice (Taylor, 2003) and to develop knowledge (Rolfe *et al*, 2001). Therefore, portfolios can enhance personal learning and development (Orland-Barak, 2005), as well as being important vehicles ensuring continued registration.

Product and process

Orland-Barak (2005) made a distinction between portfolios as 'products', and portfolios as 'processes'. A portfolio which is a 'product' acts as a tool to represent the products of learning and can be used as evidence

3

for re-registration, while a portfolio which is a 'process' can be used to demonstrate the process of learning through doing, and thereby help people to evaluate their practice. Swallow *et al* (2006) explored this idea to show how portfolios can develop practice-based knowledge for a profession. They noted that the content of portfolios is developed within the context of work and by finding solutions to problems that are not just the responsibility of the individual but of the profession as a whole. They described ways in which the examination of such work-based learning could raise people's awareness of developing new insights on practice and therefore enhance the professional knowledge base. Swallow *et al* (2006) were particularly interested in Eraut's understanding of 'process knowledge', which involves five types of process that contribute to professional action:

- Acquiring information
- Skilled behaviour
- Deliberative processes, such as planning and decision making
- Giving information
- Meta-processes for directing and controlling behaviour.
  (Eraut, 1994; Swallow *et al*, 2006)

It is easy to see how reflections about, for example, assessment procedures, clinical reasoning, providing information to patients, and analysing team working could be helpful in understanding individual practice. Then, through comparing and contrasting with the reflections of others, these reflections can be used as a means of turning tacit knowledge (that which is known but hard to articulate) (Eraut 1994) into more formal propositional or codified knowledge. Such learning can be regarded as a continuing process and with the support of managers can have mutual benefit for both the individual and organisation in which work takes place (Swallow *et al*, 2006).

Broadly then, portfolios should provide a record of an individual's professional development, i.e. the process through which practitioners can demonstrate appropriate behaviour and the ability to deal competently with practice. This involves maintaining and updating skills on an individual level. However, as a professional, individuals also have a responsibility to uphold the competence of the profession as a whole. This requires an understanding of the context in which practice occurs, an appreciation of healthcare needs and how these may change over time, and the ability to evaluate the contribution that the profession can make towards fulfilling these needs. To be effective, individuals need to be able to look critically at their performance within their organisation of practice, recognising strengths, identifying limitations and planning ways in which discrepancies can be addressed. The most recognised way of enhancing such evaluation is through a process of self-reflection.

Reflection

The concept of reflection (considered in more detail in *Chapter 8*) is based on principles of adult learning, including the idea that individuals need to be self-motivated and prepared to use work-based experiences to form concepts and generalisations that can be applied in new situations (Dewey, 1933; Kolb, 1984; Dagley and Berrington, 2005). However, reflection is not easy and takes time to undertake effectively. Orland-Barak (2005) highlighted the difficulty of converting an experience into a theoretical basis for future action and noted that while intellectual skills are required, so too is the ability to appraise any potential emotional impact. She identified the language particular to reflection, which was based on the work of Hatton and Smith (1995). Within this language system there are four levels of reflection:

- **Descriptive writing** — a practical dimension, which includes reports of events or literature
- **Descriptive reflection** — an ethical dimension, which provides reasons based on personal judgement
- **Dialogic reflection** — a more critical dimension, which is a form of discourse with oneself and an exploration of possible reasons
- **Critical reflection** — a transformational dimension involving reasons given for decisions or events, which take account of the broader historical, social or political contexts.
  (Orland-Barak, 2005)

In her study of portfolios used in teacher education, Orland-Barak found that there was a predominance of the descriptive levels of reflection at the expense of more interpretive, dialogic or critical levels (Orland-Barak, 2005). One of the suggested ways to develop reflective skills more effectively, is to involve others in the process — the use of assessors, colleagues or mentors is widely recommended (Pitts *et al*, 2002; Orland-Barak, 2005; Swallow *et al*, 2006; Austin and Braidman, 2008). It should be noted that portfolio content tends to be personal and should be honest if it is to achieve results — this may present a challenge as the disclosure of weaknesses or mistakes can be uncomfortable. However, this can easily be solved by dividing the portfolio into sections that the individual is prepared to share with others and sections that are to remain confidential (Swallow *et al*, 2006).

Another challenge that faces practitioners, according to Swallow *et al* (2006), is the potential conflict between different perceptions of practice. Some practitioners, professional regulatory bodies or employers may focus on competency-based practice, bound by rules and protocols. This so-called 'technical-rationality' model is likely to involve 'tick-box' achievement of skills, which might leave underlying values and norms unchallenged. The alternative 'professional artistry' model allows practitioners to be more reflective and intuitive, enabling them to reconsider the value of theories in use and challenge assumptions (Swallow *et al*, 2006). One way to enhance the more critical, interpretive and transforming types of reflection among practitioners is to introduce the concept early during the educational process, so that it becomes internalised as a necessary part of development.

Portfolios in education

Portfolios are used both formatively and summatively in professional education (McMullan *et al*, 2002). Buckley *et al* (2009) conducted a systematic review of the evidence for educational effects of portfolios on undergraduate student learning. They looked at 69 studies from medicine, nursing and allied health professions, including occupational therapy and physiotherapy. In all professional groups portfolios were used mainly in the clinical setting, completion was mostly compulsory, reflection was required and assessment (formative, summative or a combination of both) was the norm. Students were mainly required to keep a portfolio for one academic year or less. Buckley *et al* (2009) found that the evidence base for the educational effects of portfolios is limited. Most of the studies involved student or tutor views of the effects of portfolio use on their learning. Very few studies reported direct observation of changes in knowledge, skills or attitudes/behaviours, although students reported improvements in their independent learning, decision making, critical thinking, communication, self-confidence and professionalism. Notwithstanding these limitations, the higher quality studies suggested benefits to student reflection and awareness, knowledge and understanding and preparation for postgraduate training in which the keeping of a portfolio is important (Buckley *et al*, 2009).

The recommendations provided for successful implementation of undergraduate portfolios are as follows:

- To realise the benefits to student learning, it is important that:
  - The time demands of the portfolio are reasonable
  - Support is in place to build students' reflective skills, particularly in the early stages of portfolio use
  - Undergraduate portfolios reflect as far as possible the requirements of postgraduate training
- To ensure reasonable time demands, portfolios should:
  - Have specific aims and objectives that are well understood by tutors and students
  - Align to course outcomes
  - Include clear guidelines on requirements, word limits and expected time commitments
- To develop students' reflective skills, portfolios should:
  - Be used for as long a duration as practicable, to allow skills to improve over time.

(Buckley *et al*, 2009)

Creating a professional development portfolio

There is no single format for a professional development portfolio but it is likely to include:

- Biography
- Professional roles
- Appraisal recommendations
- Learning needs identified
- Personal development plans/learning contracts
- Continuing professional development activities
- Evidence to support the outcomes of learning.

(Jasper and Fulton, 2005; Dagley and Berrington, 2005)

When used selectively, CPD 'tools' (including SWOT analyses and critical incidents; see *Chapters 2 and 3*), can help to identify appropriate learning needs, reflect on experiences within the workplace, provide evidence for the learning outcomes and demonstrate personal growth and professional development.

Checklist for a professional development portfolio

Alsop (2000) has provided a useful checklist to help formulate a professional development portfolio. It is important to ask whether or not the portfolio:

- Presents evidence carefully selected according to the purpose of the professional development portfolio
- Presents evidence in a structured way
- Shows how evidence is to be interpreted in the light of any assessment criteria
- Sets the evidence in the context of personal goals
- Presents information that is well-ordered, indexed, and cross-referenced, so that information can be found quickly and easily by other readers
- Presents material concisely, comprehensively, clearly and neatly
- Demonstrates reflection, analysis, critical awareness, and self-evaluation
- Indicates learning outcomes from various experiences
- Shows how learning and new knowledge are being, or will be, applied in practice
- Indicates plans and the direction of future development activity.
  (Alsop, 2000)

Samples of the recommended formats for doctors, occupational therapists, physiotherapists and speech and language therapists can be found on the following websites:

http://www.gmc-uk.org	General Medical Council
http://www.cot.co.uk	College of Occupational Therapists
http://www.csp.org.uk	Chartered Society of Physiotherapists
http://www.rcslt.org	Royal College of Speech and Language Therapists

Other professional bodies may have their own recommendations.

What are CPD activities?

The list of activities from which learning can be derived is wide-ranging and without limit. Nevertheless, regulatory bodies usually provide some advice — for example, the HPC (2010) has offered some useful suggestions about what form CPD activities can take, under the following headings:

- **Work-based activity** — which could include case studies, audits or secondments
- **Professional activity** — which could include involvement in a professional body, lecturing or teaching
- **Formal education** — which could include courses or writing articles
- **Self-directed learning** — which could include reading journals or reviewing books
- **Other activities** — which could include voluntary work. See the Health Professions Council (2010) for a more comprehensive list.

What counts as evidence?

Regulatory and professional bodies usually comment on the need to provide evidence within portfolio material and may provide examples. The HPC (2010), for example, categorises evidence under three sections:

- Materials you may have produced, such as information leaflets, critical reviews or procedural documents
- Materials showing you have reflected on and evaluated your learning and work, such as evaluations of courses or conferences attended
- Materials you have received from others, such as testimonies or letters from service users.

Wilkinson *et al* (2002) highlight some appropriate points to consider, which although aimed at doctors, apply equally to all health professionals:

- Evidence should cover the domains of patient care, personal development and context management
- There should be evidence that the individual has continuously undertaken critical assessment of their own performance, identifying and prioritising areas that require improvement and taking action to enhance performance
- Evidence should be sufficient, current and authentic. (Wilkinson *et al*, 2002)

Rather than becoming too prescriptive about what constitutes evidence, it may be preferable to consider the purpose it serves. Evidence is required both to show that appropriate and relevant CPD activity has been undertaken and that development has occurred as a result. Therefore, it is insufficient to include a patient information leaflet that has been produced, without also using a CPD tool, such as a significant learning event, reflective log, or application of a learning cycle to highlight learning that has occurred as a result of completing the exercise.

The practice of accumulating documentation about CPD activities can lead to a substantial volume of material being gathered. There is usually a chronological limit to the extent of required material (for example, the HPC expects documentation covering a period of two years). Nevertheless, a system of easy retrieval of material should be considered, so that it is readily available when called upon for audit or appraisal. Some examples of how evidence might be indexed in a portfolio are given in *Table 1.1*.

Conclusion

Professional development portfolios (PDPs) are limited as they depend on the ability of the practitioner to be skilled at reflection, which takes time. Although there is much theoretical evidence to indicate that PDPs are linked with professional growth, it is too early to have accumulated strong empirical evidence to show that linking CPD to re-registration has had an impact on fitness to practise. Nevertheless, there is sufficient evidence to show that portfolios have value in providing a focus for continuous learning. Portfolios are now a mandatory adjunct to CPD activities and provide tangible evidence for the process of lifelong learning. They act as a systematic and ongoing reflection on, and documentation of, personal growth and have the potential to make an important contribution towards the development of professional knowledge.

Key points

- Portfolios are integral to clinical governance
- They enhance personal learning and development
- They may enhance practice-based knowledge for a profession
- They may benefit the individual and the organisation

Table 1.1. Record of CPD activity

Evidence number	Evidence	Category of evidence	How does this contribute to to quality of your practice and service delivery?	How does this benefit the service user?	
1[a]	Case study	Work-based	Highlights reflections on best practice	Service user more likely to receive well-considered care	
2[c]	Designing a protocol	Professional activity	Identifies appropriate standard of care	Provides consistent standard of care	
3[a,b]	Course certificate	Formal education	Skill enhancement	Service user more likely to receive skilled care	
4[c]	Action plan	Self-directed learning	Highlights discrepancies in individual's capacity to fulfil service needs	Needs are better met	

a = record of knowledge
b = record of skills
c = record of behaviour

References

Alsop A (2000) *Continuing professional development. A guide for therapists*. Blackwell Science, London

Austin C, Braidman I (2008) Support for portfolio in the initial years of the undergraduate medical school curriculum: what do the tutors think? *Medical Teacher* **30**(3): 265-271

Buckley S, Coleman J, Davison I et al (2009) The educational effects of portfolios on undergraduate student learning: A Best Evidence Medical Education (BEME) systematic review. BEME Guide No. 11. *Medical Teacher* **31**(4): 282-298

Dagley V, Berrington B (2005) Learning from an evaluation of an electronic portfolio to support general practitioners' personal development planning, appraisal and revalidation. *Education for Primary Care* **16**(5): 567-74

Department of Health (1998) *A first class service: Quality in the new NHS*. HMSO, London

Department of Health (1999) *The Health Professions Act*. HMSO, London

Department of Health (2007) *Trust, assurance and safety – The regulation of health professionals in the 21st century*. HMSO, London

Dewey J (1933) *How we think*. DC Heath, Boston, MA

Endacott R, Gray M, Jasper M, et al (2004) Using portfolios in the assessment of learning and competence: the impact of four models. *Nurse Education in Practice* **4**(4): 250-257

Eraut M (1994) *Developing professional knowledge and competence*. Falmer Press, London

Foster P, Wilding P (2000) Whither Welfare Professionalism? *Social Policy & Administration* **34**(2): 143-159

General Medical Council (2010) http://www.gmc-uk.org/ [Last accessed 5/10/11]

Glaze JE (2002) Stages in coming to terms with reflection: student advanced nurse practitioners' perceptions of their reflective journeys. *Journal of Advanced Nursing* 37 (3): 265-272

Hatton N, Smith D (1995) Reflection in teacher education: towards definition and implementation. *Teaching and Teacher Education* **11**(1): 33-49

Health Professions Council (2010) *Continuing professional development and your registration*. http://www.hpc-uk.org/publications/brochures/index.asp?id=103 [Accessed 5/10/11]

Jasper MA, Fulton J (2005) Marking criteria for assessing practice-based portfolios at master's level. *Nurse Education Today* **25**(5): 377-389

Kolb D (1984) *Experiential learning. Experience as the source of learning and development*. Prentice-Hall, New Jersey.

McMullan M, Endacott R, Gray M, et al (2002) Portfolios and assessment of competence: a review of the literature. *Journal of Advanced Nursing* **41**(3): 283-294

Nursing and Midwifery Council (2010) http://standards.nmcuk.org/PreRegNursing/statutory/competencies/Pages/Competencies.aspx [Accessed 18/10/11]

Orland-Barak L (2005) Portfolios as evidence of reflective practice: what remains 'untold'. *Educational Research* **47**(1): 25-44

Pitts J, Coles C, Thomas P, Smith F (2002) Enhancing reliability in portfolio assessment: discussions between assessors. *Medical Teacher* **24**(2): 197-201

Rolfe G, Freshwater D, Jasper M (2001) *Critical reflection for nursing and the helping professions: A user's guide*. Palgrave, Basingstoke

Simpson E, Courtney M (2002) Critical thinking in nursing: literature review. *International Journal of Nursing Practice* **8**(8): 89-98

Swallow V, Clarke C, Iles S, Harden J (2006) Work-based, lifelong learning through professional portfolios: challenge or reward? *Pharmacy Education* **6**(2): 77-89

Taylor C (2003) Narrating practice: reflective accounts and the textual construction of reality. *Journal of Advanced Nursing* **42**(3): 244-251

Tochel C, Haig A, Cadzow A, Beggs K, Colthart I, Peacock H (2009) The effectiveness of portfolios for post-graduate assessment and education. BEME Guide Number 12. *Medical Teacher* **31**(4): 320-339

Twaddle JW and Johnson JL (2007) A time for nursing portfolios: a tool for career development. *Advances in Neonatal Care* **7**(3): 146-50

Wilkinson TJ, Challis M, Hobma SO, et al (2002) The use of portfolios for assessment of the competence and performance of doctors in practice. *Medical Education* **36**(10): 918-924

Chapter 2

SWOT analysis: a tool for CPD

Introduction

Jon Larner

Of all the continuing professional development (CPD) tools available to the health professional, SWOT (Strengths, Weaknesses, Opportunities, and Threats) analysis is perhaps the most simple to use. It requires just a pen and a blank piece of paper, and involves nothing more than writing a list of your perceived strengths and weaknesses along with the opportunities and threats that you recognise within a given situation or event.

Despite its simplicity, SWOT can be a very helpful tool for focusing the act of reflection onto a specific set of circumstances. It is therefore useful as a starting point when preparing a learning strategy or tailoring CPD activities to suit your personal setting. The process of completing a SWOT analysis is helpful both for focusing your concentration onto the situation under review, and for recording key points. A SWOT analysis should be the stepping stone for producing a learning strategy or development plan, and when used in combination with other CPD tools, it can provide an excellent record of development over time.

What is SWOT?

SWOT is an acronym that refers to the headings given to the four quadrants made by drawing a large cross on a blank sheet of paper. These headings are:

*   Strengths
*   Weaknesses
*   Opportunities
*   Threats.

More recently, the term 'SWOB analysis' has become popular, where the 'T' for 'Threats' has been swapped for 'B' for 'Barriers'. This may be because a barrier seems more tangible than a threat, and can always be overcome.

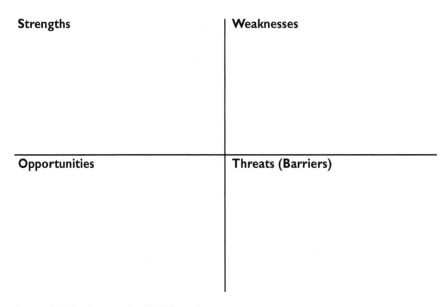

Strengths	Weaknesses
Opportunities	Threats (Barriers)

Figure 2.1. The layout of a SWOT analysis.

Although it has been used as a tool for a long time in business and marketing, it is hard to be specific about the origin of SWOT analysis as no early citations are recorded. It is generally believed to have originated at Stanmore University in the 1960s. Research led by Albert Humphrey, funded by the Fortune 500 companies, has been credited with the early development of the tool, primarily as a way to investigate what was going wrong with corporate planning at that time (Chapman, 2004). After this it became increasingly popular as a tool for stimulating business development, or 'change management' as we call it now. Others have suggested that it was developed by Harvard academics at around the same time (Panagiotou, 2003). Whatever its origins, SWOT analysis has undoubtedly been a useful tool in boardrooms for the past 50 years (Freisner, 2010).

In addition to its obvious appeal in the business world, the use of the SWOT tool has also been recognised as beneficial within the field of education. In particular, it has been identified as a simple and effective tool for students to self-analyse and to develop learning goals and priorities (Atkinson, 1998). The popularity and growth of SWOT within healthcare curricula since the 1990s probably reflects the increased profile of continuing professional development (CPD) within this field. Since the Health Professions Council (HPC) has made CPD a statutory requirement for all registrants from 2006 (Health Professions

Council, 2009), tools such as SWOT analysis are likely to become increasingly valuable as part of health professionals' CPD toolkits.

At the University of East Anglia School of Allied Health Professions (AHP) we encourage students to complete SWOT analyses at certain points throughout their studies, to map their development needs. This is particularly helpful before starting a new clinical practice placement and can be repeated after the placement to review progress. It may also be helpful for practice educators who are new to the experience of taking students, who wish to identify areas for development.

How to do a SWOT

Like all good tools for CPD, SWOT is remarkably simple. It has the advantages of being quick and easy to produce and it provides a clear record of how you were feeling at a particular time. It should also help to crystallise your thoughts by prompting you to look objectively at a situation or set of circumstances (Atkinson, 1998). It is always sensible to clearly identify the target of your SWOT analysis — by specifically considering what you are analysing, your reflection will be more focused. Otherwise, there is a risk that the findings will be too generalised and therefore harder to break down into strategic actions at a later stage. If it is to have any real value, it is critical that the analysis is an honest appraisal of your thoughts but the information included may relate to any aspect of professional, academic or personal life.

Johari's Window

A good level of self-awareness is critical for preparing a SWOT analysis. Therefore, before beginning your SWOT, it may be helpful to consider a conceptual model that represents what you know about yourself. Ever since it was first described by Joseph Luft and Harry Ingham in 1955, the Johari's Window model has been widely used for this purpose (Shenton, 2007). This model features a box divided into four quadrants, like panes of a window (*see Figure 2.2*). Each pane represents an area of knowledge about an individual and these 'panes' are presented in a two-by-two matrix. The x-axis considers what is known and unknown to the self and the y-axis considers what is known and unknown to others.

	Known to self	**Not known to self**
Known to others	**Quadrant 1** Area of free activity	**Quadrant 2** Blind area
Not known to others	**Quadrant 3** Avoided or hidden area	**Quadrant 4** Area of unknown activity

Figure 2.2. Johari's window (Luft and Ingham, 1955).

Quadrant 1 of the Johari's Window model recognises that for any individual, there will be behaviours and motivations known to both self and others. The model refers to these as 'free activity'. Knowledge in this quadrant will often form a significant part of our developmental activity as we can address these learning needs openly with others. When we openly receive and acknowledge feedback from others about our performance, this quadrant can yield valuable information for our SWOT analysis.

Quadrant 2 recognises a 'blind area', where other people can see things about us of which we are unaware. It is impossible to acknowledge this in a SWOT analysis, and to develop strategies to address these issues, until we are made aware of the knowledge within this quadrant. Frequently asking for feedback from others will help us move knowledge from Quadrant 2 into Quadrant 1, where it can be acknowledged in our SWOT analysis and used in a meaningful way.

Quadrant 3 acknowledges an 'avoided or hidden area' which is the part of ourselves that we know well, but keep hidden from others. There may be many reasons for this but often this quadrant contains information that needs to be more openly acknowledged in order to develop strategies and improve. It may be necessary for us to share part of this information with key people (such as supervisors and mentors) in order to make our strategies more meaningful.

Quadrant 4 identifies that for every person there is an area of 'unknown activity' where both the individual and others are unaware of certain attitudes, behaviours and motives. We know that these exist because later they can begin to emerge and it becomes evident that they have been influencing us for some time (Luft, 1969). While they remain unknown, it is not possible to consider them in your SWOT analysis.

The Johari's Window can be a helpful model for developing self-awareness. It encourages us to reflect on what we know about ourselves and to seek more insight into that which is unknown. When developing a SWOT analysis it is likely that strengths and weaknesses will be drawn from what we already know about ourselves (Quadrants 1 and 3). In order to develop meaningful strategies for personal and professional development, we should be encouraged to share information from our hidden area (Quadrant 3) with supervisors and mentors. However, there will always be some information that we choose to keep private. In contrast, opportunities and threats may well involve the exploration of areas that are initially unknown to us (Quadrants 2 and 4), which begin to emerge as we engage with CPD activities.

SWOT — an example

In the School of Allied Health Professions, we encourage students to complete a SWOT analysis before and after each of their practice placements. The example below relates to a student therapist, who is about to embark on her first practice placement (see *Figure 2.3* overleaf). Having prepared the page by dividing it into appropriate quadrants, the student considers each quadrant in turn.

Analysing SWOT quadrants

You will note that the statements under 'strengths' and 'weaknesses' relate specifically to the student, whereas those under 'opportunities' and 'threats' generally refer to the external environment. This is important as it allows individuals to consider their perceived strengths and weaknesses in light of the unique external opportunities and threats that present themselves at that moment in time. The process of writing these things down can be useful in itself, and can bring them to the forefront of your thinking. Nevertheless, to really make the most of a SWOT analysis, the individual should develop a strategy or action plan to:

- Build upon the strengths
- Manage the weaknesses and, where possible, turn them into strengths
- Capture and make the most of the opportunities
- Minimise or work around the threats/barriers.

Figure 2.3. An example of a student's SWOT analysis.

Strengths	Weaknesses
Good communication with people	I tend to get anxious about my ability to succeed, I lack confidence
I am keen to learn, interested and prepared to work hard	I can be quiet when feeling nervous, and slow to speak up
My previous work experience as a therapy assistant	I lack confidence when formally presenting information to others
I am flexible and adaptable to new situations	I sometimes have unrealistic expectations of myself
I am open to constructive feedback	

Opportunities	Threats (Barriers)
To learn some of the skills needed to become a therapist	Difficulties with child care arrangements
Chance to look at role models in action	Previous work experience as a therapy assistant
To put some of the skills I have learnt so far into action	Risk of finding it tiring working and coping with children at night
Chance to test myself, gauge progress	Not keeping on top of homework

Let us refer back to *Figure 2.3* which features a real student example of a SWOT analysis. It is interesting that this student identified her previous work as a therapy assistant as both a strength and a threat. It was perceived as a strength because of the body of prior knowledge and experience that the student had received from this role. However it was also perceived as a threat because the student was genuinely concerned that others may make assumptions about her level of knowledge and experience. After completing the SWOT, the student's strategy was to discuss this openly with her clinical supervisor at the start of the placement to clarify her level of previous knowledge/experience.

In a similar way, the student identified that her tendency to have unrealistically high expectations of herself was a weakness. However, her first practice placement was also seen as an opportunity to gauge performance and to find out whether or not her expectations were appropriate. In this case, the resultant strategy was for the student, together with her practice educator, to set small, realistic goals. These were then transferred to a learning contract which could be evaluated both during and after the practice placement.

Using the SWOT analysis to track CPD over time

While a SWOT records what you are thinking there and then, there is potential value in carrying out a series of SWOTs at different times. These can then be compared, as they will have recorded changes in your perceptions of the four parameters over a period of time. A 'before and after' SWOT can be helpful for measuring how things have changed over a specified time period or during a particular event.

The most effective way to demonstrate your learning is to record your strategies, or action points for how you intend to manage the issues raised in your SWOT. This involves the identification of learning objectives, which can be recorded on a learning contract, and specific resources that may be required to address these objectives. The formation of a strategy, based on your SWOT, which includes appropriate action points and learning goals will act like a road map directing you to a successful outcome. Although the SWOT analysis is an essential part of the process, it is usually the strategy that provides the blueprint for change. It is beneficial to clearly identify a timescale for addressing each of the goals set out on your strategy (Smyth, 1996). A final point to remember is that different tools can be used in conjunction with each other. For example, a SWOT analysis might be used as a precursor for a learning contract (*see Chapter 4*), which then identifies your learning objectives and becomes your action plan.

Conclusions

A SWOT analysis is a simple tool that individuals can use to reflect upon their perceived strengths and weaknesses within the context of a specific situation. These factors are considered in the light of the unique set of opportunities and threats that present themselves at that moment in time. The process of completing a SWOT analysis will help focus the act of reflection and will provide a record of key points. However, the SWOT analysis also has the potential to be a powerful tool for mapping CPD over time, when repeated periodically and linked through the use of accompanying strategies or action plans. If used in combination with other tools such as learning contracts, it can be a valuable addition to the CPD toolkit.

Key points

- In order to engage in meaningful CPD, it is important to have a clear understanding of your developmental needs
- SWOT analysis provides a simple, structured way to analyse your developmental needs
- SWOT analysis helps individuals to document their strengths and weaknesses within the context of the external opportunities and threats specific to the situation under review
- SWOT analysis can clearly signpost areas that require specific action and should act as a prompt for the development of a learning strategy or developmental plan
- Johari's Window can be a helpful conceptual model for developing self-awareness. It encourages reflection on what we know about ourselves and also encourages us to seek greater insight into that which is unknown
- SWOT analysis can be used to map CPD over time and when used alongside strategies or action plans, can plot progress and highlight patterns or themes for future development

References

Atkinson (1998) SWOT analysis: a tool for continuing professional development. British *Journal of Therapy and Rehabilitation* **5**(8): 433-435

Chapman A (2004) *SWOT analysis methods and examples.* Available online at: http://www.businessballs.com/ [Accessed: 9/11/2010]

Freisner T (2010) *History of SWOT Analysis.* Available online at: http://www.marketingteacher.com/swot/history-of-swot.html [Accessed: 23/08/2010]

Luft J (1969) *The Johari Window: A Graphic Model of Awareness in Interpersonal Relationships, Reading book for human relations.* Available online at: http://www.library.wisc.edu/edvrc/docs/public/pdfs/LIReadings/JohariWindow.pdf [Accessed 16.06.2011]

Panagiotou G (2003) Bringing SWOT into focus. *Business Strategy Review* **14**(2): 8-10

Shelton A K (2007) Viewing information needs through a Johari Window. *Reference Service Review* **35**(3): 487-496

Smyth T (1996) *Managing Health & Social Care.* Macmillan, London

The Health Professions Council (2009) *Continual professional development annual report.* HPC publications, London

Chapter 3

Using critical incidents to enhance CPD: student perspectives

Introduction

Chia Swee Hong and Anne Guyon

Reflection is a fundamental component of continuing professional development (CPD). This chapter focuses on critical incident analysis — a tool that supports reflective practice. Critical incidents can be used to explore the links between theory and practice and provide strategies for coping with similar incidents in the future. They can also be used as part of a personal portfolio/profile. In this chapter, case studies are presented, by a physiotherapy student, occupational therapy students, and a speech and language therapy student, which demonstrate the use of critical incidents for reflection.

Critical incidents (sometimes referred to as 'significant learning events') may be positive or negative experiences. Benner (1984) suggests that critical incidents range from the ordinary and typical, to events that went unusually well or that were particularly demanding.

According to Lillyman and Evans (1996), critical incidents are those that have made some emotional impact on us. In order to learn, it is not enough to simply experience a critical incident. To help learning and development take place, we must also reflect on the incident. Gibbs (1988) adds:

> *This learning must be tested out in new situations. The learner must make the link between theory and action by planning for that action, carrying it out, and then reflecting upon it, relating what happens back to the theory.*

This is supported by Tripp (1993) who stated, 'critical incidents are produced by the way we look at a situation, it is an interpretation of the significance of the event' (Ghaye and Lillyman, 2006).

When used selectively, critical incidents can help us analyse experiences, identify learning outcomes and demonstrate our growth and professional development. The process of reflection can help to dissipate the emotional response which may result from a difficult experience. It is suggested that where these tools are used regularly and when the process is documented, as in writing-up a critical incident, we are able to build up a portfolio of evidence demonstrating professional development.

Critical incidents

When asked to reflect on a critical incident, most of us are likely to raise the following questions:

- What is it?
- How do we do it?
- What do we do with it?

These are normal responses, as without support, reflection is a difficult task (John, 1994). Holm and Stephenson (1994) point out that there are no firm rules for the best way to reflect on one's practice, but with experience we are gradually able to build our own framework. The choice of tool will depend on the type of experience being reflected on and is likely to be influenced by the individual's learning style. However, a list of questions can be a useful guide to help us focus our thinking on critical incidents. For example, Cross (1997) asks us to consider the following four questions:

- What is the critical incident?
- What did I learn?
- How did I acquire the learning?
- How have I applied this learning in my practice?

A personal communication from Coles (Alsop, 1995) suggests asking:

- What was the nature of the experience or event?
- What aspects of the event went well, or what was good about the experience?
- What did not go so well or was not so good?
- What were my feelings about what happened?
- What were the feelings of others?
- What have I learnt from the experience?
- What did others think I should learn?
- What do I need to do next?
- How can I use what I learned in professional practice?

However, we must take care to avoid reducing our experiences to merely answering a series of questions 'that splinters the human encounter' (John, 1994). The questions above should be used as an *aide memoire* to structure our experience in a meaningful way (Cross, 1997).

According to Ghaye and Lillyman (2006), 'it is the analysis and evaluation of the experience that can then be used to improve clinical practice, apply scientific knowledge and ultimately develop and provide evidence of an expert practitioner'.

Without documenting the incident, it may be lost from memory with no evidence of learning or development. Furthermore, writing can provide an objectivity in relation to the initial learning experience (Walker, 1985). Finally, Holm and Stephenson (1994) maintain that reflection has assisted them to become more aware of the need to question the validity of their own and other's actions in relation to practice, stating that, 'reflection enables us to find clarity and conclusion in the midst of confusion and conflict.'

The following case studies give examples of critical incidents documented by allied health professional (AHP) students, identifying how and where these can be applied to practice.

Case study 1: First year speech and language therapy student

Describe what happened

For one hour every week I visit my conversation partner, a patient who has suffered a stroke. Following his stroke, he had developed aphasia and he sometimes finds communication difficult.

At my third independent visit he spoke in depth about his stroke, openly discussing how it had occurred and how it had affected his life. He was able to tell me the exact date and time that it had occurred (he obviously had experience of describing the episode) and he explained that it had affected his life in many different ways. He expressed a great desire to be able to change things such that he could return to the active, career-driven lifestyle he had before the stroke. He mentioned that he sometimes felt unhappy and dissatisfied with his life. We discussed the things that he missed the most and his hopes to continue with his DJ and music career.

What were your thoughts and feelings? How has it affected your confidence? What anxieties or concerns did it cause?

Having only met him on a small number of occasions, I was extremely nervous about listening to him talk about an event that had such a severe impact on his life. I found it difficult to listen to him talk about the stroke and how he felt about his current situation — it was obvious that he was unhappy about parts of his life and I was unsure how to react. I also found it difficult to get the right balance and be sympathetic towards him without appearing patronising. The situation was difficult for me to connect with as I have had no previous experience of communicating with someone who has suffered a stroke and I have not been through this experience myself.

How did it affect the patient and/or other people? How did the patient react? How did this affect the patient's treatment? Were there other people involved or affected by the incident?

My conversation partner appeared to be at ease when talking about his stroke. It was obvious from his relaxed manner and openness that he had talked about it before, and he was able to freely discuss the impact that it had on his life.

I was unsure how to react to much of his conversation and this led to uncomfortable silences between us. However, this did not affect our relationship or subsequent conversations.

What was good and bad about the situation? Was the overall experience positive or negative? What positives and negatives can be drawn out of the experience?

On reflection, I did not react in the right way — when he spoke about the stroke and its impact on his life I was unable to communicate my feelings and I did not bring any prior knowledge of stroke to the conversation.

However, after writing a reflective log and reflecting on the situation, I came to view the experience as a positive one overall. Listening to my conversation partner talk about his experiences helped me to understand some of the serious after-effects that strokes can have and how they can change people's lives. The experience also made me realise that in my profession I would be dealing with people who are facing difficult times and experiencing things that may be life-changing.

What sense can you make of the situation? Why do you think this situation arose? How can you ensure that the positive aspects are repeated and the negative aspects are avoided in future?

I was aware that the situation would arise at some point during my placement, as one of the objectives was to learn more about aphasia and stroke sufferers. However, I was unaware that my conversation partner would feel comfortable enough to share his experience so early on in the placement. In future, I will avoid the negative aspect of not knowing how to react by talking to my conversation partner advisor and asking their advice on how to deal with this type of situation. More positively, I now have a greater knowledge of aphasia and stroke sufferers and will be able to carry this into my professional career and future conversations on the topic.

What learning or development needs has this highlighted for you? What action points do you draw out of this situation for yourself? Is there a gap in your knowledge? Do you need more training?

The action points I drew from this situation were based around my lack of knowledge and experience of the subject. To help develop my knowledge, I asked my conversation partner advisor for advice. I was also able to share my experience with others who were on placement, gain feedback and find out how they dealt with similar situations.

Case study 2: First year occupational therapy student

When assisting an occupational therapist to hoist a patient, I identified a lack of confidence and experience with moving and handling. The apprehension I felt before the event indicated that I did not feel capable, despite having had the relevant training. This was exacerbated by other weaknesses such as avoidance of things I am not very good at. The embarrassment that I felt following a mistake I made during the hoisting prompted me to write up a 'significant learning event' based on Alsop (1995), to break the event down in a meaningful way in order to structure my reflection and maximise my learning.

What was the event?

I was assisting an occupational therapist in hoisting a patient between a bed and a chair on a hospital ward, to assess whether or not it would be appropriate equipment for the patient to have at home and if so, to determine which size sling they would need. It was a quick assessment and I was to help in the absence of another member of staff being available to do so.

What did not go very well?

I felt apprehensive about assisting the occupational therapist to do this because I had little experience of doing so and was not confident. I was hesitant and felt that I was not much help. At one point I wrongly applied the brake when it should have been left off (the patient was being lowered into the chair) and this could have caused the chair to tip back, putting the patient at risk. This was very unprofessional and may have decreased the patient's confidence in the occupational therapy service.

What did go well?

I felt that I appropriately acknowledged my apprehension and lack of experience with the occupational therapist, both before and after seeing the patient. This was important as it enabled them to judge what role would be appropriate for me to take and it also ensured that they were vigilant for the safety of all involved. I also felt that discussing my weakness in this way was a personal achievement.

How did I feel?

I was embarrassed that I had made such a mistake and that despite having had the training, I was not confident in what I was doing. However, I was pleased that I did not make a scene in front of the patient and that I discussed my feelings with the occupational therapist.

How did others feel?

The occupational therapist was very understanding and explained that this is simply one of those things that takes a lot of practice. She reassured me that over time I would develop confidence and competence with moving and handling. I got the impression that the occupational therapist did not consider the situation to be as significant as I did.

What have I learned?

I have learned that I cannot assume that I will always remember everything. It is important that I revise, practise and reflect on techniques before implementing them, so that I do not put anybody at risk and so that I can be of valuable assistance. If I am unsure of what I am doing, then I should definitely acknowledge this with fellow staff, to ensure that I do not put anybody at risk. I can then learn and develop my skill set to reach my full potential. Teamwork is vitally important to keeping a professional approach in front of patients.

Case study 3: Second year physiotherapy student

This is an occasion that I believe demonstrates my professional behaviour.

When did it occur?

During the fourth week of my most recent placement in a specialist neurological hospital.

Who was involved?

A patient who I had cared for since the beginning of my placement, my clinical educator and myself.

What happened?

The patient had been involved in a road traffic accident in which he sustained damage to the frontal lobe of his brain. This resulted in a dense hemiplegia and some behavioural difficulties, which included physical and verbal abuse (such as kicking, punching and swearing) and the constant repetition of words such as 'it hurts', 'home' and 'bed'. These behavioural difficulties presented frequent challenges when working with him.

During one physiotherapy session, he seemed to be more agitated than normal and his behaviour was particularly challenging. The session proceeded with relative success but we reached a point where my clinical educator and I had to stop, because the patient's behaviour was putting us at risk of being hurt. Although the patient had initially been doing well with the tasks that we were working on, he gradually became less compliant to a point where it was not beneficial for the patient or for us to continue.

At this point I asked the patient why he was trying to hurt us and he said that it was because he was scared. I then asked him what it was he was scared of and to this he replied 'dying'. I explained that he wasn't going to die, and that he was in good health at the moment. I told him that he was in good hands and that we were working to make him as well as possible before he went home. I then encouraged him by talking about how well he had been doing during the session and how pleased his mum and dad would be when I told them about his progress. We went on to joke about the cheesy grins that he had made to the camera and discussed showing the pictures to his mum and dad.

When the patient said that he was scared of dying, I was quite surprised because it was unusual for him to show much insight into his condition. I wasn't expecting to have to deal with conversation about life, dying and his condition. However, I consider my reactions to this situation to have been very professional, and there are a number of aspects of my behaviour that stand out.

Aspects of my behavior which I consider to be professional

- **Verbal and non-verbal communication** — I used these skills to reassure and console the patient. I found the correct words to use and then delivered them clearly and sensitively, at an appropriate level so as not to appear disrespectful or patronising. I also used physical contact and eye contact to gain greater trust and put the patient at ease.
- **Rapport and people skills** — I knew that I had to be understanding and serious in my approach but I also found the right time to make a joke about events earlier in the session, in order to lift the patient's spirits.
- **Responsibility for the situation** — In our department, one therapist is designated the lead for each session. This is to remove unnecessary stimuli and to help maintain their attention. For this session, I had taken the lead and although my clinical educator was present and had experience at dealing with such situations, I took responsibility for the discussion with the patient.

I have chosen this event as an example of professionalism as it demonstrates my ability to handle difficult and sensitive situations and highlights some behavioural attributes that it is very important for health professionals to have.

I consider the professionalism demonstrated in this event to be transferable to other situations. Although discussions about life and death are uncommon outside of certain areas of physiotherapy (such as neurology and respiratory), the ability to discuss important and sensitive issues with patients is necessary in all settings. For example, when seeing a musculoskeletal patient, I may have to talk about future job prospects or the possibility that they may no longer be able to live their life in the way that they would like to. Patients can be very sensitive about these issues and practitioners must all offer the same level of professionalism.

Throughout this placement, my ability to demonstrate professionalism has developed. This is illustrated by an extract taken from my reflective diary, which describes a situation similar to that already described. I did not handle it very well. However, I reflected on this event and developed an action plan, which I think helped me through the more recent situation.

The extract from my reflective diary is as follows:

One of the patients on the ward is expressing suicidal thoughts to a few of the staff. She is an MS sufferer and is having a relapse phase and severe spasms. Whilst there isn't a real danger of her being able to commit suicide in the hospital, she is openly voicing her wish to end her life when she is discharged. Today I walked past her room and she was crying, so I went in to see if she was all right. I found myself unable to help her, as I didn't really know what to say. All I was able to do was get a member of staff who was more experienced than me. I really hope that she doesn't voice her suicidal thoughts to me again because I am not sure how to deal with them.

Changing attitude

My attitude towards the situation described in my reflective diary was one of avoidance and apprehension as to how I would react and cope. However, I can now take great confidence from how I handled the physiotherapy session. While I am very conscious that challenging situations are unique, and that handling them effectively involves an individual approach, specific to the patient, I think that this positive learning experience has developed my professional behaviour when dealing with challenging situations. By reflecting on previous experiences, I have been able to demonstrate my ability to handle situations in a sensitive and competent manner.

To continue to develop my professionalism I must ensure that I adopt a serious and professional manner with patients and staff alike. After developing an understanding of the individual and having built the relationship that they want to have with me as a physiotherapist, I can then develop a rapport with the patient.

Case study 4: Third year occupational therapy student

During the four weeks before my placement I attended seminars on 'children with special needs', which I found quite frustrating. Except for one, all of my colleagues had already been on paediatric placements and although the content of these seminars was appropriate for all of us, I felt unable to contribute to discussions as I lacked experience that the others could draw upon. Therefore, when I had the opportunity of going on an eight-week paediatric placement, I was thrilled. I believed that I would find it enjoyable and rewarding to work with lovely little children, and that it would be very different from working with an elderly client group.

Throughout the first week I felt like a small fish in a very large pond. I was very much an observer, standing on the periphery of groups. My supervisors encouraged me to 'interact' with the children but I had not imagined how difficult this would be. When I watched the other staff interacting so well with them, I felt inadequate. I was surprised that I felt so intimidated by the children. On one occasion, I tried to speak with a little boy who was playing with some beads — I introduced myself, but he didn't even acknowledge my presence and I left the session feeling totally defeated and a complete failure. I hadn't realised that communicating with children would be so different from normal conversation. For several days after this, my experiences in paediatric occupational therapy continued to be negative.

However, my confidence increased dramatically following an experience during the second playgroup, which I consider a critical incident. My supervisor asked me to carry out an occupational therapy assessment on a girl with cerebral palsy. I enjoyed the challenge that had been set, and it forced me to think on my feet as I put my knowledge into practice. I instinctively used toys and games to assess the child's abilities, and it suddenly occurred to me that this is the role of occupational therapy in paediatrics — to select activities which promote the development of specific skills, and then to continually assess the child's progress by observing them playing.

Although this seems obvious now, I was not really aware of it during the first couple of weeks as I was concentrating on getting used to being among children. Following the incident, my confidence grew and I became involved in planning and running activities — some went better than others. After only eight weeks I cannot claim to know all that there is to know about paediatric occupational therapy. However, by reflecting on the experiences that I have had on this placement, I think I have gained a better understanding of occupational therapy and I have begun to develop some of the skills that are needed to address the unique problems of each child.

The professional development module has given me an opportunity to explore learning processes and I have learned a number of things about my personality and preferred styles of learning, which will help me continue to learn after I qualify. I find that I learn best when I identify a critical incident, which I can then investigate in the literature. Relating this knowledge back to practice feeds into the reflective cycle of learning — reflection is playing an increasingly important role in my personal and professional development.

I find that my interest and motivation to learn are increased when I am able to amalgamate theory and practice in the context of a situation — the process of discovery through action. I will be able to continue this pattern of learning as a basic grade occupational therapist by reading and discussing books and journals to increase and update my theoretical knowledge. I will grasp every opportunity to attend relevant courses and workshops and I shall continue to keep a reflective diary, as I have found this particularly useful during my paediatric placement. It will encourage me to think more about what I am doing, to challenge my practice and to become more competent. The final important thing that I have learned during this module is that confidence is synonymous with knowledge and understanding. I feel that my confidence has increased so much because I have taken every opportunity to learn new skills and acquire new knowledge.

Through reflection, I have gained a deeper understanding of myself and the practice of occupational therapy. As I approach the next stage in my career, I realise that my journey of discovery and development has only just begun.

Conclusions

Critical incidents can be used to enhance CPD, by turning difficult experiences into learning opportunities, and they may be used as part of a personal portfolio/ profile. They can be used to explore the links between theory and practice and provide strategies for coping with similar incidents in the future. The examples presented in this chapter have shown that the analysis of critical incidents can facilitate both professional and personal development.

Key points

- Reflective practice enables us to examine and evaluate current practice and identify what is being learned, what should remain the same and what needs to change
- Reflective practice is best supported by a range of tools such as clinical reasoning and critical incident analysis. When used selectively, these strategies can help us reflect on experiences, identify learning outcomes and demonstrate our growth and professional development
- Critical incidents are those that have made some emotional impact on us. The experience may be either positive or negative
- Critical incidents may be used as part of a personal portfolio/profile. They can be used to explore the links between theory and practice, and to provide strategies for coping with similar incidents in the future
- Without documentation, an incident may be lost from memory and there may be no evidence of learning or development. Furthermore, writing encourages objectivity in relation to the learning experience

References

Alsop A (1995) The professional portfolio — purpose, process and practice (part 2). *British Journal of Occupational Therapy* **58(8):** 337–40

Benner P (1984) *From novice to expert: Excellence and power in clinical nursing practice.* Addison Wesley, California

Cross V (1997) The professional development diary — a case study of one cohort of physiotherapy students. *Physiotherapy* **83(7):** 375–83

Ghaye T, Lillyman S (2006) *Learning journals and critical incidents.* Quay Books, London

Gibbs G (1988) *Learning by doing.* FEU, London

Holm D, Stephenson S (1994) Reflection — a student's perspective. In: Palmer A, Burns S, Bulman C (eds) *Reflective practice in nursing.* Blackwell Science, Oxford

John C (1994) Guided reflection. In: Palmer A, Burns S, Bulman C (eds) *Reflective practice in nursing.* Blackwell Science, Oxford

Lillyman S, Evans, B (1996) *Designing a personal portfolio profile: A workbook for healthcare professionals.* Quay Books, London

Tripp, D (1993) *Critical incidents in teaching.* Routledge, London

Walker D (1985) Writing and reflection. In: Boud R, Keogh R, Walker D (eds) *Reflection: Turning experience into learning.* Kogan Page, London

Chapter 4

Learning contracts in practice: their role in CPD

Introduction

Jon Larner and Anne Guyon

For centuries, scholars have pondered over the way that adults learn. In the pursuit of our understanding of this process we have developed a range of theories, models and principles that underpin adult education (Merriam, 2001). Authors such as Malcolm Knowles recognised that as they mature, learners become more self-directed, and for decades educators have tried to identify the best ways to assist this transition to self-directed learning, seeking to find the best fit between educational activities and the needs of individual learners (Jones-Boggs Rye, 2008).

Knowles described self-directed learning (1975: p18) as a process:

...in which individuals take the initiative, with or without the help of others, in diagnosing their learning needs, formulating learning goals, identifying human and material resources for learning, choosing and implementing appropriate learning strategies, and evaluating learning outcomes.

He proposed that proactive learning through the use of one's initiative is much more effective (in terms of quantity, quality and retention of information) than more reactive, traditional, didactic styles of learning. The learning contract is founded upon this important education principle.

During the 1980s and 1990s, there was a steady increase in the adoption of learning contracts into healthcare education programmes (Martenson and Schwab, 1993; Cross, 1996; Lowry, 1997). This has been credited to a number of perceived benefits, including increased motivation and excitement to learn, greater flexibility and the promotion of a wider range of learning resources and strategies (Solomon, 1992; Tomkins and McGraw, 1988; Knowles, 1990). When the objectives have been achieved, learning contracts offer rewards, which may be extrinsic (praise) or intrinsic (a sense of achievement) (Bastable *et al*, 2011). Cross (1996: p21) recognised that learning contracts fit well with the demands of healthcare training courses, such as physiotherapy, which demand 'personal involvement, self-initiation and self-evaluation, combined with a sense of mutual respect and collaboration'. Cross also acknowledged that affinity with the process of developing professional autonomy has made learning contracts popular across all healthcare education courses. Matheson (2003) identified that student occupational therapists found learning contracts helpful in providing structure to their learning, identifying knowledge and remaining client-centred in their approach. McAllister and Lincoln (2004) recommend learning contracts as a means of mapping learning objectives on speech and language therapy placements. They also suggest that educators use them to map their own development through the placement experience.

What are learning contracts?

Learning contracts have been defined by numerous authors. Solomon (1992: p205) defines them as:

> *...an agreement between a learner and an educator that specifies in detail: learning objectives; the resources and strategies required to accomplish the objectives; the evidence required to demonstrate the objectives have been accomplished; and the specific criteria for evaluation.*

Although the learning contract is centred on the principles of self-directed learning, it also involves a collaborative approach between two parties. These two parties might be a student and a placement educator, although they could just as easily be a qualified clinician and a manager. For the purposes of this chapter the term 'learner' is used to describe the person who carries out the contract, and the term 'mentor' describes the person who facilitates this process. Collaborative learning places the emphasis on the generation of knowledge rather than the transmission of knowledge (Jones-Bloggs Rye, 2008: p1475). This means that students take responsibility for identifying their learning objectives and then discussing them with their supervisor. This is instead of the educator simply telling the student what their learning objectives should be. Although the latter often seems the simplest and quickest way of learning for the student, research into adult learning tells us that we learn and retain information much better when we work it out for ourselves.

The word 'contract' suggests a formal agreement between the learner and the mentor. However, in practice this works most effectively as a negotiation process that allows for a dynamic, flexible learning environment and that promotes the acquisition of self-directed skills (Solomon, 1992: p205). Tompkins and McGraw (1988) summarised this process as a '...continuously renegotiable working agreement'.

It is important to recognise that both parties have responsibilities within the learning contract. While the learner should be self-directed and provide the drive and creativity, the mentor also has an important role to play. When describing the mentor's role, Solomon (1992: p205) emphasises the importance of recognising the clear shift from imparter of knowledge to facilitator of learning. This is necessary if the learner is to express him or herself and become self-directed, as described by Knowles. This shift is mirrored in other areas of healthcare education, where students are expected to take greater responsibility for their learning and there is less reliance on more traditional, didactic styles of teaching (Whitcombe, 2001). For students, this process can help them to develop the skills required for lifelong learning (Solomon, 1992). This also makes the learning contract a particularly powerful tool for clinical placement education as it enables the learner to take responsibility for clarifying the purpose, process and outcomes of a learning experience (Walker, 2004). Nevertheless it is important that the use of a learning contract is not seen as an easy option to remove pressure from the mentor (Lowry, 1997). It should be remembered that there may be institutional and educational requirements, which may need to be taken into consideration when drawing up a learning contract (Jarvis, 2004).

A learning contract form used in the School of Allied Health Professions, University of East Anglia, is shown in *Figure 4.1*.

Developing a learning contract

The development of a learning contract involves a series of steps, which are described in *Table 4.1*. These steps have been adapted from Alsop (2004) and Anderson *et al* (1996).

Identify a relevant learning need

The first step of the process is to establish appropriate learning needs upon which the contract will be focused. To avoid ambiguity, the learner needs to be clear of the contract's purpose. A good example is the use of a learning contract to guide and measure a student's learning outcomes from a practice placement.

Student		Educator		
Date Agreed		Date Due		
Learning Goal	Strategies	Resources	Evidence	Achieved
Signature of Student		Signature of Educator		

Figure 4.1. Fieldwork learning contract, as used in the School of Allied Health Professions, University of East Anglia.

Ideas can be pooled from a variety of sources — in this case they might include lectures, discussion with peers, competency standards and discussion with placement educators. It is worth noting that learners may not find this process straightforward, particularly when new to the process or if used to more traditional teaching methods (Yeung *et al*, 2001). Discussion with the mentor can be helpful and will help to align the learner's perceived needs with ones that are appropriate to their stage of development (Walker, 2004). It is also important to acknowledge that this process may be time-intensive (Matheson, 2003).

Establish learning goals or objectives

There is a saying in the business world that 'what gets measured gets done' (Cameron, 2010). Applying the same thinking to learning goals can help us to make effective progress in achieving them. This is important as it is not uncommon for students to set themselves generic and ambiguous aims that are hard to measure (Yeung *et al*, 2001). The development of a learning contract requires learners to distil their learning needs into precise statements that provide the focus for learning strategies. These goals or objectives may be concerned with the acquisition or improvement of professional skills and knowledge. They may also focus on aspects of professional development such as communication skills

Table 4.1. Steps involved in developing a learning contract

Identify relevant learning needs
Establish learning goals or objectives
Specify strategies for achieving outcomes and resources required
Determine suitable evidence for demonstrating a successful outcome
Clarify the means of assessment and validation of the evidence
Establish timeframe for completion of contract
Review the contract
Carry out the contract
Submission and self-assessment — evaluation of outcomes against recorded criteria
Identify future learning needs

or record keeping. It is also possible that the learner may wish to focus on less tangible emotions or feelings, such as confidence. In this case it is essential that the learner thinks carefully about how the objective will be measured. It might be that this refers to observable behaviours that can be assessed, but it is important to avoid generic statements such as 'I want to improve my confidence'.

It is important that goals are specific, measurable, achievable, realistic and time-defined (SMART). They should be appropriate to the learner's stage of professional development, the available resources and the timescale involved. As there is always the potential to learn more, it is not uncommon for learners to include too many objectives. This is usually linked to the erroneous belief that they should know absolutely everything about a particular topic or area (Walker, 2004). Therefore, it is important that the mentor is quick to reinforce the necessity for SMART objectives (Yeung *et al*, 2004) and to emphasise the importance of quality rather than quantity when it comes to learning. Although this process is time-consuming, the time spent at this stage will save time at a later date when the learner is looking for evidence of achievement.

Specify strategies for achieving outcomes and resources required

Learners should consider methods of learning that best suit their own learning styles (Bastable and Doody, 2011). This may be influenced by the nature of the goal, the setting and available resources (Matheson, 2003) — resources are defined as 'available means of support' (Allen, 2008, p434). These may include books and journals, professional standards and guidelines, colleagues, seminars and conferences, case notes, personal diaries, librarians and mentors. Initially the learner may need help to identify appropriate resources and also to access them, if they are working in a new and unfamiliar environment (Walker, 2004). Discussion between mentor and learner is important to ensure that the learner's expectations are realistic.

Determine suitable evidence for demonstrating a successful outcome

It is important that the learner carefully considers what evidence is required to convince him or herself and others that the learning objectives have been achieved. This is best considered when the objectives are first set (Walker, 2004) and encourages learners to think carefully about how they will show that they have reached the desired standard. This may be about demonstrating skills and knowledge, achieving specific clinical outcomes or recognising the behaviours and attitudes expected of them. Ideally the evidence should include a range of different types of activity appropriate for measuring the learning objective. This could include personal reflections, relevant written work or study, supportive statements and validation from others. Examples of completed evidence include:

- Practical demonstration of skills with feedback
- Presentation of case studies with feedback
- Review of evidence-based practice
- Written reports or essays
- Reflective diary extracts and significant learning events
- Anonymised clinical notes or treatment records.

Clarify the means of assessment and validation of the evidence

Once appropriate evidence of achievement has been established, the learner and mentor need to agree upon suitable criteria for evaluating each of the objectives — clearly stating the criteria for evaluation will prevent ambiguity at the end of the process (Walker, 2004). These criteria must be sensitive enough to evaluate the level that the learner has attained. There may be occasions where the opinion of someone with specialist experience, who is not directly involved in the contract, is needed. This should be flagged up within the resources required for completion of the contract.

Establish timeframe for completion of contract

It is important that the learning contract clearly states the expected completion date. This may occur at a natural boundary of progress such as the completion of a placement, or the achievement of a broad aim. This will allow learners to set realistic, achievable objectives and to prioritise their time appropriately (Tompkins and McGraw, 1988). It will also prompt learners and their mentors to arrange suitable times to review the contract and monitor progress, e.g. the midway point of a placement.

Review the contract

After completing a draft of the learning contract it is sensible to leave a period for reflection — usually about a week is suitable (Walker, 2004). This is necessary for the learner to check that the contract matches the original intention(s). This can be done individually or with colleagues who may offer a new perspective. The following checklist may be helpful in structuring this reflective time:

- Are the goals or objectives SMART?
- Are there additional strategies or resources that should be considered?
- Does the evidence seem relevant and appropriate to the various objectives or intentions, and is it convincing?
- Is there other evidence that might be considered?
- Are the criteria and means for validating the evidence clear and relevant?

Carry out the contract

With the learning contract completed, the learner is able to fully engage with the learning experience and to begin to address each of the objectives. The amount of ongoing supervision will depend on the learner's individual needs — it is important to note that changes can still be made at this stage, in consultation with the mentor. Learners are advised to regularly review their progress against each objective throughout the learning experience, but it is important that both mentor and learner formally review progress at the halfway stage and at other mutually agreed points during the process (Alsop, 2004).

Submission and self-assessment – evaluation of outcomes against recorded criteria

When the learning contract is completed it may be used as a checklist by the learner. If all previous stages have been well planned and carried out then this will be relatively straightforward. Learners should take responsibility for the learning that they have undertaken by asking themselves if the stated goals have been met and whether or not there is suitable evidence to demonstrate this. An example of a contract completed by a UEA student is included in *Figure 4.2.*

Identify future learning needs

Although the contract may have fulfilled its main purpose at the end of a specific learning experience, its value extends beyond this as it can help to clarify future learning needs. Rarely in life do we come away from a learning experience with all our objectives successfully completed and nothing to address in the future. Students completing a practice placement will undoubtedly have objectives to carry forward, either because they have not been able to fully address them or because their learning is expected to mature as they advance through their studies. This can apply equally to qualified practitioners as they engage with lifelong learning (Solomon, 1992). A learner needs to be motivated to identify strategies for their continual professional development (Jones-Boggs Rye, 2008) and a learning contract can act as a road map for the next stage of this journey.

Advantages and disadvantages of learning contracts

Anderson *et al* (1996) list the following advantages of learning contracts:

- They are individual to the learner, therefore increase motivation
- They are flexible, thus can be tailored to suit the individual's learning style and pace of learning
- They encourage self-directed learning
- They bring a sense of ownership to the learner's activities and to the learning process.

In addition to these points, Matheson (2003) and Whitcombe (2001) found that

Student			Educator	
Date Agreed			Date Due	
Learning Goal	Strategies	Resources	Evidence	Achieved
Be aware of and ensure safe practice at all times.	Check and prepare before and after seeing patients. Read medical notes and collect all relevant information. Check and prepare environment. Explain everything to patient. Complete risk assessment. Don't be afraid to take control or speak up if I feel a situation is unsafe.	Medical notes and relevant information sources. Members of the MDT (updates, handovers, advice and help if required). The patients themselves (ask for regular feedback). My educator (supervision, advice and clarification that my actions are appropriate). Books and articles on key conditions and safety aspects. Organisation risk assessments.	No issues of concern. Achieve safe and successful treatments at all times. Feedback from my educator. Patient responses and achieving joint goals. Completed and signed off risk assessments. Reflective diary accounts. Significant Learning Events.	✓

[continued overleaf.]

Figure 4.2. An example of two goals from a learning contract, completed by a University of East Anglia student.

Learning Goal	Strategies	Resources	Evidence	Achieved
Improve time management, efficiency and organisation.	Complete a SWOT analysis with learning strategy and action plan. Communication: don't worry about asking/ telling others. Write in notes immediately after seeing patients; if not possible, write key words. Leave patients to do independent exercises if safe. Give patients time, come back if busy. Stay focused on task.	Learning strategy and action plan (from SWOT). Lists and cue cards to refer to. Prioritisation list, negotiated with educator. Patients and educator (written plan of what want to do before I see each patient, negotiated goals). The MDT (suggested time limits and targets from other staff members, to use as a baseline). Educator and seniors (clear set of directions for myself). Medical notes (reviewed in a timely manner).	SWOT analysis pre-placement and post-placement. Learning strategy with evaluation of achievements. Meet time limits and targets. ABC system on list. Written plan at start of each day. Achieve plan within working day. Feedback from my educator. Achievement of all patient goals set within the agreed time frame. Feedback from all of the people involved.	✓

Signature of Student   Signature of Educator

Figure 4.2 [cont.]

occupational therapy students valued the structured framework provided by a learning contract and felt that it improved communication between all parties involved. Walker (2004), quoting Dart and Clarke (1991), also identified that learning contracts encourage a deep approach to learning, thus facilitating understanding of knowledge rather than taking a surface approach that promotes rote learning.

It is important to note, however, that learning contracts also have some disadvantages, which should be acknowledged to ensure that they are used appropriately. Failure to adequately orientate learners and mentors to the process of using a learning contract can lead to anxiety and frustration (Cross, 1996). Learners who are new to this process may find the initial flexibility of learning contracts stressful, especially if accustomed to a learning environment that is didactic in nature, where the student has a more passive role. Mentors will also need to familiarise themselves with the process of implementing learning contracts and it may be useful to discuss their roles in a workshop setting, especially if they themselves are accustomed to 'traditional' education (Walker, 2004). At a fieldwork educators' workshop session on implementing learning contracts, clinical educators expressed concerns regarding use of the word 'contract' (Walker, 2004). To reduce any preconceived ideas of a rigid, formal contract, the process of negotiation between the mentor and the learner must be emphasised. Highlighting the importance of negotiation will also help to alleviate another concern voiced by both educators and participants, that the learners may have unduly high expectations of resources, which might not be available. Lowry (1997) suggested that problems may occur if there are personality clashes between the parties involved. In such cases, more than one mentor should be available to carry out the contract. Perhaps the most consistently raised concern about learning contracts is that the process is time consuming (Solomon, 1992; Whitcombe, 2001; Matheson, 2003). Mentors have identified time limitation as a disadvantage of contracts, compared with other teaching strategies, especially when first implemented (McAllister, 1996). This may be related to either the mentor or the learner being unfamiliar with the process. Certainly students who are unaccustomed to taking an active role in their learning will need additional support from their mentors (Walker, 2004).

Conclusions

A learning contract provides a means of encouraging learners to take responsibility for their own learning objectives and therefore promotes a sense of ownership over professional development. It can be used at any stage of a learner's professional career and across a wide variety of learning environments. This flexibility makes the learning contract a valuable tool for self-directed learning and continuing professional development. Implementing learning contracts may be a new skill for learners and support is advised when they are initially introduced. Similarly, mentors who are unfamiliar with the process may benefit from attending relevant workshops.

Acknowledgements
The authors would like to acknowledge the previous work of Elizabeth Walker during her time as a lecturer at the University of East Anglia, School of Allied Health Professions. They would also like to thank all those who have participated in practice educator workshops and conferences at the UEA and provided valuable insight into the use of learning contracts in practice. Finally they would like to thank all of the students who regularly share their experiences and allow us to continue to develop our teaching and learning strategies for future students.

Figure 4.1 is redrawn with kind permission of the School of Allied Health Professions, University of East Anglia.

Key points

- Learning contracts are derived from the ideas of educators, who believe that what adults choose to learn on their own initiative is learned more deeply and permanently than in 'traditional' education, where the learning process is structured primarily by the teacher and the institution
- Learning contracts encourage self-direction, thus enabling learners to control their learning experiences to meet their own needs and develop skills to educate themselves
- Stages involved in developing a learning contract include: identify relevant learning needs; establish learning goals or objectives; specify learning strategies and resources; determine the evidence of accomplishment; clarify the means of assessment and validation of the evidence; establish the timeframe for completion; review the contract; carry out the contract; submission and self-assessment; and identification of future learning needs
- Learning contracts take into account individuals' different learning styles and pace of learning

- Implementing learning contracts may be a new skill for learners, hence support may be necessary when they are initially introduced
- Similarly, mentors who are unfamiliar to the process may benefit from attending relevant workshops
- The flexibility of learning contracts makes them a useful tool for CPD

References

Allen R (2008) *The Penguin pocket English dictionary.* Penguin, London

Alsop A (2004) *Continuing professional development: A guide for therapists.* Blackwell Publishing, Oxford

Anderson G, Boud D, Sampson J (1996) *Learning contracts: A practical guide.* Kogan Page, London

Bastable SB, Gramet P, Jacobs K, Sopczyk (2011) *Health professional as educator: Principles of learning and teaching.* Jones and Bartlett Publishing, Sudbury, MA

Brookfield SD (1996) *Understanding and facilitating adult learning.* Open University, Milton Keynes

Cameron S (2010) *The business students handbook: Skills for study and employment.* Prentice Hall, Harlow

Cross V (1996) Introducing learning contracts into physiotherapy clinical education. *Physiotherapy* **82**(1): 21–7

Dart B, Clarke J (1991) Helping students become better learners: A case study in teacher education. *Higher Education* **22**(3): 317–35

Jarvis P (2004) *Adult education and lifelong learning* 3rd edn. Routledge Falmer, Oxon

Jones-Boggs Rye K (2008) Perceived benefits of the use of learning contracts to guide clinical education in respiratory care students. *Respiratory Care* **53**(11) 1475–81

Knowles MS (1975) *Self-directed learning.* Association Press, New York

Knowles MS (1990) *The adult learner: A neglected species.* 4th edn. Gulf Publishing, Houston, Texas

Lowry M (1997) Using learning contracts in clinical practice. *Professional Nurse* **12**(4): 280–3

Martenson D, Schwab P (1993) Learning by mutual commitment: Broadening the concept of learning contracts. *Medical Teacher* **15**(1): 11–15

Matheson R (2003), Promoting the integration of theory and practice by the use of a learning contract. *International Journal of Therapy & Rehabilitation* **10**(6): 264–70

McAllister L, Lincoln M (2004) *Clinical education in speech language pathology.* Whurr, London

McAllister M (1996) Learning contracts: An Australian experience. *Nurse Education Today* **16**(3): 199–205

Merriam SB (2001) Andragogy and self-directed learning: Pillars of adult learning theory. *New Directions for Adult and Continuing Education* **89**(Spring): 3–13

Solomon P (1992) Learning contracts in clinical education: Evaluation by clinical supervisors. *Medical Teacher* **14**(2/3): 205–10

Tompkins C, McGraw M-J (1988) The negotiated learning contract. In: Boud D ed. *Developing student autonomy in learning* 2nd edn. Kogan Page, London: 172–91

Walker E (2004) Learning Contracts in Practice: Their role in continual professional development. In: Hong CS, Harrison D eds. *Tools for continual professional development.* Quay Books, Dinton

Whitcombe SW (2001) Using learning contracts in fieldwork education:The views of occupational therapy students and those responsible for their supervision. *British Journal of Occupational Therapy* **64**(11): 552–8

Yeung E, Jones A, Webb C (2001) The use of learning contracts. In: Kember D ed. *Reflective teaching and learning in the health professions.* Blackwell Science, Oxford

Chapter 5

Utilising broadcast media as a means for enhancing CPD

Introduction
Martin Watson

The UK has a long-standing reputation for the high quality of its public broadcasting, including the transmission of materials which are tacitly or overtly 'educational'. Historically, this has been epitomised by the radio and television output of the British Broadcasting Corporation (BBC) and the Open University (which until 2006 delivered learning materials to its students via BBC transmissions). A wealth of material is now available via radio, and to some extent television, which has the potential to inform and facilitate learning for allied health professionals (AHPs).

The aim of this chapter is to provide a brief overview of how broadcast media can make potentially useful contributions to an AHP's continuing professional development (CPD). This is not intended as an excuse for health professionals to indulge in excessive amounts of television viewing. This chapter simply recognises that all potential opportunities for enhancing CPD should be acknowledged and, where feasible, utilised.

Although written with UK-based health professionals in mind, it is hoped that much of what is identified here will be of use to readers outside of the UK. In any event, recent advances in digital technology and the internet mean that some broadcast media are now available worldwide. While this chapter focuses on BBC broadcasting, it should be noted that other broadcasting organisations make useful contributions.

How can engagement with broadcast media support CPD?

There are at least three ways in which broadcast media can be used to inform and support a health professional's CPD. These are:

* **To keep abreast of current affairs (specifically news and information relating to recent health and social care developments)** — health professionals have a tacit responsibility to keep in touch with current

developments, and broadcast media provide an efficient means of doing so. It is readily acknowledged that the introduction of digital media has increased the speed, volume and ease of communication. Furthermore, news and current affairs programming can keep AHPs informed of relevant changes in national health policy, Government legislation and health-related scientific developments.

- **To provide information of personal/professional interest, relating to aspects of health and social care** — a broad range of radio and, to some extent, television programmes can be considered useful learning resources, relevant to AHPs, for example, listening to the BBC Radio 4 programme 'Case Notes', which provides a regular half-hour focus on current health issues. See Appendix for more examples.

- **Experiential learning** — purists argue that most (if not all) CPD activities involve experiential learning, focusing largely on self-initiated, self-driven and self-evaluated professional developmental activities. However, a specific form of experiential learning is implied here, albeit a vicarious one. When talking about a specific aspect of nursing CPD, Edwards (2007) makes the following comment: 'Experiential knowledge includes gaining inner personal meaning from life experiences. Nurses have personal experiences such as having a baby, bereavement or a close family member spending a period of time ill in hospital. These experiences develop experiential learning, which can form part of an individual nurse's knowledge to draw on in clinical situations' (p.310).

  Broadcast media may provide an additional means by which vicarious experiential learning can occur, as many programmes have the potential to provide meaningful insights into the 'lived experience'. This might relate to the experiences of individuals with specific medical conditions, or those who live with (or have had to help manage) people with these conditions. To give an example, a television series exploring the experiences of people with a physical disfigurement (the author is following one at the time of writing, http://www.channel4.com/programmes/katie-my-beautiful-friends) may offer useful insights to health professionals who encounter people living with a disfigurement — for instance, therapists involved in the management of burns patients. In a much broader sense, broadcast media have the potential to offer insights into a wide range of personal/professional development issues, regardless of any explicit relation to health and social care.

Alsop (2000) makes the point that 'CPD embraces many…activities through which individuals learn and develop their skills and expertise. It includes informal learning and on-the-job learning and can also include forms of both intended and incidental learning' (p.1). This acknowledges that CPD activities can be fortuitous. For instance, many health professionals will listen to the radio without consciously paying attention to their personal development needs, but such activity can lead to useful insights and reflections.

Identifying what's 'on', not missing programmes of interest and finding the time to listen and view: when do I do all this?

We know that both planned and fortuitous interactions with broadcast media can contribute to CPD, but how do we engage with broadcasting? A simple answer would be to watch television and listen to the radio as often as possible! The following are suggestions for focused and purposeful engagement:

- **Make a note of when potentially interesting and relevant programmes are to be broadcast** — this can be done by regularly scanning a newspaper's television and radio section, or checking a weekly listings magazine (such as the *Radio Times* or *TV Times*). This information is also available via websites (e.g. www.radiotimes.com and www.whatsontv.co.uk), which can often be customised to deliver information on specific types of programming. It may be worth exploring the various electronic ways in which you can be alerted to new programmes and broadcasting schedules. For example, internet browsers can be set up to receive RSS feeds ('really simple syndication', often referred to as 'web feeds') from broadcasting companies, Twitter alerts may inform us of new programmes and smartphone applications ('apps') offer phone-based access to broadcast listings.

- **Capture or retrieve relevant programmes for viewing or listening at your convenience** — a variety of web-based applications, such as BBC iPlayer (see Appendix for more details), enable viewers to watch or listen to broadcasts at times of their choosing, using internet-connected computers or televisions. If you have the necessary hardware, an alternative strategy is to record broadcasts with a digital video recorder (DVR) or a digital audio broadcasting (DAB) radio for later viewing or listening.

The advent of podcasts has further increased access to (and the amount of) broadcast materials. While MP3 players (such as the iPod) are primarily considered entertainment devices, their potential role in CPD should not be overlooked. Radio and television broadcasts can be obtained via the internet, stored on these devices and then accessed at a convenient time, and it is even possible to customise podcast software (such as iTunes) to download and save your favourites automatically. Some broadcasters, including the BBC, are working to make past radio programmes available in podcast archives, which further increases the amount of available material.

• **Look for useful missed opportunities to engage with broadcast media** — while it is important that you have good quality leisure time, you will likely be able to identify wasted opportunities for engagement. An example might be a work-related journey. A potential strategy for making the most of this time is to listen to radio programmes via iPod/car radio.

Smythe (2004) reminds us that our best thoughts and reflections often come at the oddest (or perhaps not so odd?) times, such as when driving or when waking up. In her own words, 'the fertile ground of thinking lies in the times when the mind is resting' (p.330). For some, listening to the radio when going about routine tasks at home or when driving may provide the best opportunity for engagement.

Purposeful engagement with broadcast media: documenting one's engagement and demonstrating the use of broadcast media as CPD

As well as there being a professional expectation to engage in CPD activities, AHPs working in the UK are required to demonstrate such engagement in a tangible and verifiable way to their regulatory body. Since 2006, UK Health Professions Council (HPC) registrants have been required to record their CPD activities in a portfolio and if selected for audit, they are further required to complete a CPD profile.

A drawback of using broadcast media for this purpose is that it can be something of a chore — few professionals will be willing to spend extensive amounts of time documenting their every engagement with CPD-relevant broadcast media. Bourne *et al* (2007), in their evaluation of the CPD activities of community physiotherapists, identified that 'recording CPD achievements' was 'often' or 'very often' considered a problem. Yet documentation remains important.

There are ways in which recording can be done in a concrete, purposeful and time-efficient manner.

For portfolio, profile and possibly audit purposes, it may be sufficient to simply identify that you are involved in 'regular updating of knowledge via systematic engagement with broadcast media'. The HPC gives 'updating your knowledge through internet or TV' as an example of CPD, under the heading 'self-directed learning' (p.27) (Health Professions Council, 2010). If additional background information is required, you may reference this chapter and the strategies outlined herein.

If more specific detail is needed, then it may be useful to compile a list of programmes that you typically engage with, or perhaps keep a rolling list of specific programmes that you have recently listened to or watched. This can include brief notes on how each programme has contributed to your personal or professional development. For UK-registered AHPs this can be done during working hours, forming a part of your regular work-based CPD.

For more formal, structured and detailed CPD, you might complete a learning event log for reflective practice. While the author does not propose that this should be done for every broadcast encountered, it may prove useful in some instances. It can also provide an illustrative example, should you be selected for audit. The following sub-headings are suggested:

- Programme title, source, timings, the date it was transmitted or seen/heard
- Was viewing/listening planned or fortuitous?
- Give a brief summary of the programme (no more than a short paragraph) and/or provide a link to the programme's website (if available)
- How does viewing/listening relate to a current CPD objective?
- Give a brief summary of the specific contribution(s) this programme has made to your personal/professional development
- Identify any further action(s) (and if relevant, deadlines) resulting from viewing/listening to this programme.

Concluding comments

Similarly to the internet, information that is obtained through broadcast programming will not always be reliable. Much of the material within broadcast media is 'lightweight' and may be either factually inaccurate or incomplete. It should also be acknowledged that many supposedly 'educational' broadcasts put greater emphasis on entertainment than on detailed factual delivery. Many programmes that are seen or heard with professional intentions will ultimately do no more than trigger interest in a topic. However, as the quality of public broadcasting remains high, this will hopefully initiate further research.

As a final note, readers are reminded of the benefits of sharing good practice. To take full advantage of this (essentially free) CPD resource, you should inform your colleagues if you have accessed or know about a potentially useful programme.

Example 1: radio programme

Programme details: title; source; timing; date transmitted or seen/heard

'Metaphor for Healing', a BBC Radio 4 programme originally broadcast on the 28th October 2009.

Was viewing/listening planned or fortuitous?

I became aware of this programme after it was broadcast. Having read a complimentary review, I listened to it using the 'listen-again' facility on the Radio 4 website (while it was still available).

Give a brief summary of the programme (no more than a short paragraph) and/or provide a link to the programme's website (if available)

Dr Phil Redmond talked about how people can use words/metaphors to describe aspects of their pain/symptoms, diagnosis or treatment during a clinical consultation. A main point seemed to be negative metaphors that have sometimes been (inadvertently?) used by clinicians when describing aspects of a patient's diagnosis or treatment, e.g. 'crumbly' spine; 'toxic/burning' chemotherapy. Patients may then, in turn, inherit those negative metaphors, to detrimental effect, or may even have developed negative metaphors of their own, with similar detrimental effects on their progress and recovery. If such negative metaphors can be avoided, and/or if patients can be helped to develop more positive metaphors, then this can sometimes have very positive effects on recovery/progress and management of the patient's condition. (This is similar to the positive visualisation model which I think we're all aware of now, relating, for example, to cancer care. However, it goes beyond that, covering the needs for us as clinicians to take more care with the words/terms/stories we use with our patients, as well as being more observant about the words/metaphors/stories that patients use.)

How does viewing/listening relate to a current CPD objective?

I didn't listen to this with a specific CPD objective in mind, other than my desire to keep up-to-date with current trends/knowledge. However, aspects of this programme relate to my efforts to better understand brain function — for instance, the differences between 'left' and 'right' brain were mentioned in the programme.

Give a brief summary of the specific contribution(s) this programme has made to your personal/professional development

This programme has opened my eyes a little more to something I was only partly aware of. I was probably intuitively aware of some of the programme's content already, but (among other things) had not appreciated that some very specific and useful work is being done in this area. Hence, my actions (documented below).

Identify any further action(s) (and if relevant deadlines) resulting from viewing/hearing this programme

I have identified two areas to explore with further reading:

- Dr Graham Brown's work on the therapeutic 'reframing' of metaphors used with patients
- The work of so-called 'clean language practitioners' — a therapeutic movement which I think focuses on the very deliberate and strategic use of language we use with clients, to beneficial therapeutic effect.

Example 2: television documentary (using a significant learning event reflection tool)

What happened?

I watched a BBC 3 documentary filmed by soldiers in Afghanistan. This included their own footage taken during combat and more recent interviews with the soldiers, who were very frank and open about their feelings. I thought that the combat footage was very explicit and distressing. One of the soldiers was killed, and the programme also included interviews with his family. Threaded throughout the documentary, a letter — written to the dead soldier's family immediately after his death — was read aloud by the lieutenant who wrote it. While the soldier's family were tearful and emotional, his fellow soldiers came across as very matter-of-fact. However, towards the end of the documentary, when reading the letter's closing passages, the lieutenant became choked with tears.

What I felt about it

I have recently started to work as a volunteer with injured soldiers, so this film was very poignant. It offered some insight into the ways in which injured soldiers react to their injuries and the special needs that they have in rehabilitation. What I found particularly significant, was the realisation that their feelings about combat are very complex. The extreme levels of physical discomfort and emotional uncertainty are hard to comprehend but the soldiers adapt and cope. The most important element of coping is the social support from their comrades and a strong sense of purpose. One of the soldiers explicitly stated that going into battle and engaging in fire with the enemy was the only time that he really felt alive. This became more so after they lost one of their company and wanted to avenge his death. When life is stripped away to these bare and elemental drives, there seems to be a sense of occupational purpose like no other.

What was positive/negative about the event?

The documentary was like a good ethnographic research project, with firsthand narrative accounts and multiple sources of evidence. It was absolutely fascinating to watch and a real privilege to get such insight into the lives and feelings of the soldiers. Their bravery was stunning on many levels. The negative aspect was the distressing nature of the experiences described, and I found the combat footage terrible to watch. Their attempts to save the wounded soldier and carry him to be picked up by helicopter were particularly upsetting.

What I have learned?

This documentary helped me to understand a little more about what it is like to go into combat, and to realise the dynamics behind the challenges of adjusting to life outside the army. To regain that sense of being challenged to the limit with a group of comrades who would lay down their lives for you is hard to replicate in civilian life, particularly with a life-changing injury.

What I will do differently

I will include reflections on this documentary in my teaching about PTSD and highlight specific challenges for soldiers who have been in combat. In my voluntary work, I will continue to support injured soldiers who feel the need to undertake extreme and foolhardy challenges.

Key points

• Broadcast media (specifically radio and television) can, with judicious use, be useful and legitimate CPD resources
• Health professionals should ideally have a clear purpose in mind when engaging with these media as part of CPD, and also recognise that fortuitous engagement can sometimes yield benefits
• Users must be aware of the various means by which broadcast media can now be accessed
• Users should be familiar with the range of tools which can be used to document the use of broadcast media as part of CPD

References

Alsop A (2000) *Continuing professional development: A guide for therapists.* Blackwell Science, Oxford

Bourne JA, Dziedzic K, Morris SJ, Jones PW, Sim J (2007) Survey of the perceived professional, educational and personal needs of physiotherapists in primary care and community settings. *Health and Social Care in the Community* **15(3):** 231–7

Edwards SL (2007) Critical thinking: A two-phase framework. *Nurse Education in Practice* **7(5):** 303–14

Health Professions Council (2010) *Continuing professional development and your registration* (Revised), Health Professions Council, London. Available from http://www.hpc-uk.org/assets/documents/10001314CPD_and_your_registration.pdf)

Smythe EA (2004) Thinking. *Nurse Education Today* **24(4):** 326–32

Appendix: Some useful links and websites

This is not intended as an exhaustive list. It focuses mainly on output from the BBC (particularly Radio 4), but hopefully offers some useful suggestions:

All in the Mind A radio programme dealing with matters relating to human psychology and mental health (www.bbc.co.uk/programmes/b006qxx9)

Am I Normal? A radio programme discussing various aspects of health and wellbeing (www.bbc.co.uk/programmes/b007v7py)

Case Notes A medical programme which explores a different topical subject each week, with the help of experts, often including those with the medical problem being discussed (www.bbc.co.uk/programmes/b006th1n)

The Food Programme Some of the food-related issues discussed in this programme are certainly health-related, particularly for professionals with an interest in healthy diet (http://www.bbc.co.uk/programmes/b006qnx3)

Health Check Looks at global health-related issues (www.bbc.co.uk/worldservice/science/2009/03/000000_health_check.shtml)

Material World Provides a weekly update on scientific matters — some of these topics are health-related (www.bbc.co.uk/programmes/b00txj8l)

The Moral Maze This discusses the ethical aspects of topical current affairs matters, including those relating to current health and social care issues (http://www.bbc.co.uk/programmes/b006qk11)

Thinking Aloud Laurie Tayor's weekly exploration of social science, which provides useful insights into aspects of human behaviour (www.bbc.co.uk/programmes/b00txhtz)

You and Yours This radio-based consumer affairs programme has regular features of relevance to health professionals and those with health and ability issues (http://www.bbc.co.uk/programmes/b006qps9)

For readers wishing to revisit previous recent UK television (and to some extent radio) broadcasts, the following web-based applications may be useful:

BBC iPlayer: www.bbc.co.uk/iplayer

ITV Player: www.itv.com/itvplayer

Channel 4 On Demand: www.channel4.com/programmes/4od

Channel 5 Demand 5: www.channel5.com/demand5

Chapter 6

Peer observation: a tool for CPD

Introduction

Deborah Davys and Vivienne Jones

Peer observation is a form of peer review within teaching; a partnership in which colleagues observe each others' practice, provide feedback and engage in a discussion aimed to promote reflection (Bell, 2002). Other objectives include the identification of strengths and developmental needs, and the formulation of an action plan for further improvement (Hammersley-Fletcher and Orsmond, 2005).

Depending on the wishes of the person being observed, feedback may focus on general performance or more specifically on teaching and learning strategies, assessment, or the achievement of learning outcomes (Hatzipanagos and Lygo-Baker, 2006). A further observation can be used to assess if intended improvements have been achieved. The process has potential benefits for both parties, since observers may incorporate observed good practice into their own teaching (Bell, 2002).

Peer support and review

Peer support is not a new concept and is a recognised model of supervision (Best and Rose, 1996). Warne (2002) defined it as a general term that may encompass any form of mutual support between people who provide useful feedback to each other. It may be used to monitor caseloads (Bannigan, 2000), review clinical reasoning skills (Clifford-Brown and Segal, 2004), and foster self-confidence and self-directed learning.

Relevance to practice

In the UK, the Health Professions Council (HPC) requires all health professionals to update their knowledge and skills in order to practise effectively and to protect the health and wellbeing of service users. There is much flexibility in how this can be achieved, e.g. supervision, mentoring, appraisal, student supervision, peer review and reflective practice (Health Professions Council, 2006).

63

Reflection is arguably the most widely-used self-evaluation strategy for continuing professional development (CPD) (Reid and McKay, 2001) and, while this teaches self-awareness and self-correction, others argue that it lacks rigour (Best and Rose, 1996) and is subjective (Jasper, 2003). Peer observation provides the opportunity for staff at all levels to work in pairs with the aims of eliminating ritualistic practice, directing personal development and ensuring that a safe, ethical and effective service is offered to service users. Feedback from service users involved in the session may provide further objectivity to the process.

An approach to peer observation

This article will provide a format for the process of peer observation, based loosely on a variety of models used in teaching, such as that used by the University of New South Wales (2006). This process comprises the following stages, which are described in more detail below:

- Selecting an observer
- Agreement on aspects of practice to observe
- Observation
- Reflection on the experience
- Feedback
- Follow-up.

Selecting an observer

The observer should be a non-threatening individual, who has sufficient understanding of the other's role. Ideally this should be a more experienced colleague but could also be someone of broadly similar expertise and discipline (Claveirole and Mathers, 2003). Alternatively, an observer from a different professional background may provide an opportunity for inter-professional development and learning. Ultimately, the ability to give constructive feedback is the most helpful supervisory behaviour, regardless of seniority. However, the choice of observer may be dictated by staff resources or by the specific aspect of performance to be observed. The pair may decide to observe each other's performance or it can be a unilateral arrangement.

Agreement on aspects of practice to observe

The peer pair should agree in advance on what aspects of practice will be evaluated. A date should be arranged and consent gained if the session involves service users. If not already agreed at departmental level, the peer pair should set mutually agreed ground rules regarding the expectations, confidentiality and responsibilities of each party (Swain, 2007). There should however, be an agreement that any issues of concern or poor performance will be dealt with openly, especially if there are ethical implications. If formal feedback is desired, then a form can be designed or alternatively, feedback can be verbal or in note form — the emphasis is on content rather than the form of delivery.

Observation

The observer does not take an active role during the session but may make notes to aid feedback or complete an agreed form.

Reflection on the experience

Feedback can be provided immediately following the session, but it may be more beneficial to allow some intervening time for further reflection and evaluation by both parties.

Feedback

This should be a private and confidential meeting, allowing time for both parties to present their reflections and to consider strategies for further development. The potential for negative feedback and its implications for positive working relationships must be considered. With this in mind, feedback should be non-judgemental and respectful, supportive but challenging (Hunter and Blair, 1999) and fair and honest. The process should never be punitive and to best support future performance it should focus on behaviour rather than the person. It is important to get the right balance to ensure that the evaluation is not a threatening experience (Bannigan, 2000).

Having reflected on the session, the observer may recognise an opportunity to change and improve his or her own practice. It is recommended that some form of confidential record of the process be kept, and this can be used as evidence for CPD purposes.

Follow-up

A truly accurate judgement is unlikely to be achieved on the basis of a single observation and as the aims of peer observation are to learn and to improve practice, further opportunities are recommended to evaluate whether changes have taken place (Best and Rose, 1996). The time frame for follow-up evaluations can be entirely flexible to suit the needs and constraints of the peer pair.

Further considerations

Peer review is a process that requires careful management. While it has the potential to be used as a developmental tool for both individuals and departments, staff may fear that it will be used in a judgemental way (Hammersley-Fletcher and Orsmond, 2005), or as part of an agenda for managerial control. All forms of evaluation create stress, and it is likely that both parties will experience some degree of anxiety in any supervisory relationship (Sweeney *et al*, 2001). Although anxiety can be a helpful motivator in terms of realising one's potential (Bell, 2002), it can also generate resistance in staff who fear being deemed incompetent, especially if the process is imposed rather than available as a voluntary tool for improvement. The intentions behind the observation process must therefore be clear. The most beneficial approach is considered to be peer observation as a voluntary scheme for CPD purposes, with an emphasis on individual control and choice of observer (Swain, 2007).

Benefits

The practice of peer observation may benefit the individual practitioner, service and service user in various ways. Peer support and review are important influences in both the recruitment and retention of staff (Waygood *et al*, 2000). Sweeney *et al* (2001, p382) noted that newly-qualified staff in particular:

...appreciate a formal, structured and teaching-type approach to supervision.

Therefore, the voluntary opportunity to be observed and receive feedback may be helpful in developing a sense of professional competency. This could be a natural development from the process of being supervised as a student, and indeed, could be used during education in student pairings or in educator/ student partnerships, enabling students to practise giving, as well as receiving, constructive feedback.

Peer observation may also be used to promote reflection on practice at all levels, serving to enhance self-awareness and meet individual developmental needs (Hammersley-Fletcher and Orsmond, 2005). This may have particular relevance for experienced practitioners, who may find that increased expertise brings fewer opportunities for direct supervision and specific feedback.

As the peer review process involves the reflection of a colleague whose view is detached and objective, this may stimulate more effective reflection-on-action (Schon, 1987), and practice could be improved as a result of this process.

Few healthcare professionals will progress through their careers without minor performance issues at some time. If this can be recognised and accepted, it will become easier to deal with and hopefully provide a better quality service (Bannigan, 2000). Therefore peer observation can be used to recognise standards of work that are less than ideal and foster a supportive environment in which to address any such issues; as well as helping to meet the requirement for enhanced skills in supervision and mentoring, assessment and communication (College of Occupational Therapists, 2002).

Challenges

With the introduction of any process that aims to enhance quality and standards, there are issues that require careful consideration to avoid undermining the potential benefits. Two sensitive areas to consider are the relationships between observers and observed individuals, and the provision of feedback. If the observation and feedback process is diluted, it may simply become a mutually supportive praise session for friends (Hammersley-Fletcher and Orsmond, 2005). Swain (2007) claims that positive feedback alone is non-productive; it therefore needs to be objective and constructive, and it requires careful planning (Peel, 2005). Peer observation should focus on sharing and developing practice to the advantage of both parties and, ultimately, to the service user (Swain, 2007).

An additional concern for staff who participate in peer observation is that they may receive negative feedback or be deemed incompetent. According to Sweeney *et al* (2001) many therapists have a fragile sense of professional competence, which could affect their willingness to engage with such a process. This anxiety is likely to be increased if the process is imposed rather than voluntary. Some professionals consider peer observation to be undesirable, as it emphasises the issue of power balance between individuals (Hammersley-Fletcher and Orsmond, 2005). Clear guidelines and support are therefore necessary to reduce anxiety among staff and enable them to reap maximum benefit from the experience (Ellis, 2001). There is also a need for ground rules to deal with issues such as confidentiality (Swain, 2007). In addition, the provision of constructive feedback in a way that encourages and fosters improvement in practice is in itself a skill, and training in supervision is advocated for both parties (Ellis, 2001).

Time and resources

Although time and resources are the most frequently mentioned barriers to CPD, it is important to make time and set achievable short-term targets to attain or retain fitness to practice (Warne, 2002). In the equation of cost against benefit to all parties (Best and Rose, 1996), time is not a significant barrier: the peer observation process may be concluded within two hours (excluding time for personal reflection):

- Preparation: 30 minutes
- Observation: 30 minutes
- Feedback: 30–60 minutes

This equates to less than the half a day per month recommended for CPD by professional bodies such as the College of Occupational Therapists (2002). Although two members of staff are involved in the process, the use of peer observation is cost-effective and less disruptive to service provision than absence for course attendance. It also accommodates individual pace and style of learning. It is important however, to consider the amount of time required for thorough preparation, dissemination of instructions and the establishment of appropriate ground rules.

Example of peer observation in the clinical setting

Julie was an occupational therapist in a fast-paced outpatient musculo-skeletal service. Having recently supervised a student, she reflected on the contrast between the amount of feedback given to students and to experienced professionals and realised that the last time she had received any structured feedback was during her final placement, several years ago. Julie raised the idea of peer observation at a staff meeting and the team agreed to pilot it on voluntary basis for CPD and service enhancement.

Julie asked Lisa, a similarly experienced occupational therapist colleague with whom she felt comfortable, to observe her practice in a weekly hand clinic. While she was confident in her clinical techniques, Julie recognised that the frantic pace of the clinic required complex time-management skills and felt that the quality of her communication with patients sometimes suffered as a result. Lisa and Julie spent approximately 20 minutes scheduling a date and time for the peer observation to take place, and decided to focus attention on the style, pace and wording used within the clinical intervention. They agreed on ground rules, which included confidentiality and constructive honesty.

On the day of the observation, Julie gave each client a brief explanation and sought their consent for Lisa to be present. Lisa did not contribute to the interventions but sat quietly in the room and made notes, focusing on what went well, what could be improved on, and making general comments.

A week later, having had time to reflect on the situation, they met to share their feedback. Julie was apprehensive because she had asked for Lisa's opinion about an aspect of practice that she felt needed a lot of improvement. Her own opinion was that she sometimes blocked conversations with clients because time was so limited, and that the appearance of some of her splints could be improved. Lisa's supportive feedback helped Julie to see that despite her concerns she was maintaining appropriate professional standards of practice. She also gave Julie some ideas for reorganising the splinting area, which would make production faster, and suggested that some tasks, such as explaining the purpose of therapy or splinting could be delegated to a trained assistant. Julie asked Lisa if they could repeat the exercise a few months later, to evaluate how her skills had improved, and they used each others' notes as the basis for a reflection within their CPD folder. They also agreed on a date and time for Julie to observe Lisa with a focus on providing feedback about a complex assessment with a new patient.

Benefits

Lisa's feedback benefited Julie as an individual practitioner, and also the service and its clients: Julie felt her practice had been validated by the process, and was empowered to improve her work by the helpful and supportive nature of the feedback. The departmental team was able to implement simple, cost-effective measures that improved efficiency and client care. While Julie acknowledged that being observed in practice was stressful, her level of anxiety was lessened by the positive working relationship and the ground rules set prior to the observation.

Example of peer observation in an educational setting

Jane and Peter are lecturers in radiography and physiotherapy, respectively, and both are responsible for admissions to their programmes. Each academic year, all staff are required to have their teaching practice observed by a peer, and on the basis that he could understand her role and consider it from an independent perspective, Jane asked Peter to give her feedback on how she ran an open day for prospective students.

The date and time of the observation were clarified and goals set — Jane wanted feedback on her presentation style and the quality of publicity information that she provided, together with any general comments that Peter may note. During the observation, after being introduced to the delegates and his presence explained, Peter sat quietly at the back of room. Using a template suggested by the university, Peter recorded some brief notes on the aims of the session, learning outcomes to be achieved, the learners' level of engagement and the overall session plan.

It was agreed that they would meet for a reflective discussion three days later. In the meantime, Jane made her own notes using another agreed template to help her reflect on the session, including her overall evaluation of the session, aspects that went well, areas for improvement, her ability to keep to the session plan and a future action plan.

At the half hour-long feedback meeting, each gave a verbal summary of the session, following which they discussed Peter's written notes. While he thought Jane could improve the clarity and layout of one of her presentations, he positively reinforced her skills in verbal communication — particularly her ability to put members of the audience at ease and engage them.

Benefits

As the open day provided the first direct contact between prospective students and tutors, and its aim was to recruit students to a programme that was also offered by a neighbouring university, Jane was aware of the importance of making the best possible impression. Peter's feedback about her slides and documentation was helpful — while he understood the admissions process, the course-specific aspects were not familiar to him, and he was able to look at these from an independent viewpoint. He identified aspects that could be simplified for clarity, particularly in relation to course requirements and content. An unexpected benefit for Peter was that by observing Jane, he got ideas for how he might improve his own practice — Jane invited current students to field questions and he decided to make this a part of his own open day. In addition to benefiting the institution and potential students, a further positive outcome was that Jane and Peter were able to use the exercise as evidence of professional and academic CPD.

Conclusion

All health professionals registered with the HPC are expected to provide a high quality service, irrespective of their area of practice — be it clinical, managerial or educational. Therefore, health professionals need to take personal responsibility for monitoring the standard of their own work (Bannigan, 2000). Peer observation of practice has potential benefits for all practice settings and can be used as a tool for professional development for both the observed individual and the observer. The concept of peer observation is not a new one — it is used to varying degrees across all health professions but it most frequently relates to education. The process can be beneficial to all grades of staff who have undergone some training in supervision, who are able to provide each other with constructive feedback, encouraging learning through reflective practice. The process should not be imposed and it is important that the choice of pairing is left to the individuals. Used constructively, it is a valuable means of demonstrating CPD.

The benefits of adopting a policy of peer observation within a department may include increased confidence and skill for observed individuals and the opportunity for observers to implement good practice into their own work settings. Additionally, there could be positive implications for the recruitment and retention of staff, and the provision of a supportive environment in which staff can actively promote their own development and that of their colleagues.

Key points

- This chapter presents a brief background to peer observation of practice, peer review and peer support
- The relevance of peer observation of practice to healthcare professionals working at different levels within diverse contexts of practice is discussed
- A practical process to assist in the implementation of peer observation of practice is outlined
- Critical analysis of some of the issues surrounding peer observation of practice is presented
- Time and resource implications of this process are reviewed

References

Bannigan K (2000) To serve better: Addressing poor performance in occupational therapy. *British Journal of Occupational Therapy* **63**(11): 523–8

Bell M (2002) *Peer observation of teaching in Australia.* Available from: www.ltsn.ac. uk/genericcentre

Best DL, Rose ML (1996) *Quality supervision - Theory and practice for clinical supervisors.* WB Saunders Company Ltd, London

Claveirole A, Mathers M (2003) Peer supervision: An experimental scheme for nurse lecturers. *Nurse Education Today* **23**(1): 51–7

Clifford-Brown M, Segal B (2004) Peer review pilot. *Occupational Therapy News* **12(1):** 13

College of Occupational Therapists (2002) Position statement on lifelong learning. *British Journal of Occupational Therapy* **65**(5): 198–200

Ellis G (2001) Looking at ourselves – Self-assessment and peer assessment: Practice examples from New Zealand. *Reflective Practice* **2**(3): 289–302

Hammersley-Fletcher L, Orsmond P (2005) Reflecting on reflective practices within peer observation. *Studies in Higher Education* **30**(2): 213–24

Hatzipanagos S, Lygo-Baker S (2006) Teaching observations: Promoting development through critical reflection. *Journal of Higher Education* **30**(4): 421–31

Health Professions Council (2006) *Continuing professional development and your registration.* Health Professions Council, London

Hunter EP, Blair EE (1999) Staff supervision for occupational therapists. *British Journal of Occupational Therapy* **6**(8): 344–51

Jasper M (2003) *Beginning reflective practice.* Nelson Thornes, Cheltenham

Peel D (2005) Peer observation as a transformatory tool? *Teaching in Higher Education* **10**(4): 489–502

Reid A, McKay V (2001) Self-evaluation and occupational therapy fieldwork educators: Do they practise what they preach? *British Journal of Occupational Therapy* **64**(11): 564–71

Schon D (1987) *Educating the reflective practitioner.* Jossey-Bass, San Francisco

Swain C (2007) Has someone got their eye on you? *The Times Higher Educational Supplement* **9 March:**

Sweeney G, Webley P, Treacher A (2001) Supervision in occupational therapy, part 2: The supervisee's dilemma. *British Journal of Occupational Therapy* **64**(8): 380–7

University of New South Wales (2006) *Peer observation of teaching.* Available from: http://www.ltu.unsw.edu.au/content/teaching_support/peer_observation.cfm?ss=0 (accessed 25 October2007)

Warne C (2002) Keeping in shape: Achieving fitness to practise. *British Journal of Occupational Therapy* **65**(1): 219–23

Waygood S, Beavis F, Mathewson S (2000) Clinical governance at Gloucestershire Royal NHS Trust Occupational Therapy Service. *British Journal of Occupational Therapy* **63**(11): 535–8

Chapter 7

Clinical reasoning as a tool for CPD

Introduction

Richard Stephenson

Clinical reasoning is a useful tool for exploring and directing professional development. By declaring the reasoning employed during clinical problem solving, including the knowledge and skills used in such clinical episodes, therapists identify a range of personal and professional strengths and weaknesses that can guide future learning for enhanced practice.

Cognitive mapping can be used as a tool to make clinical reasoning explicit. It is postulated that through the construction and analysis of 'problem-oriented' cognitive maps, it is possible to identify an individual's strengths and deficits in the knowledge and skills used to solve a problem. Furthermore, through dialogue with a mentor or peer group, collaborative analysis of the content, underlying assumptions and the strength and source of evidence can enhance individuals' understanding of their capacity to effectively reason and manage client problems. Where this includes reflection on the therapeutic skills that are required (and not simply on what theoretical knowledge is needed), the therapist is enabled to determine areas of practice where development is necessary and to implement a plan for CPD. Where this information is used as part of appraisal, it serves as a focus for negotiated and supported activity leading to CPD.

Reasoning in clinical practice

The following analogy, which was used by Devlin (1991) to explore the logic of information, can offer an insight into clinical reasoning:

> *Consider travelling back in time to encounter an 'ironsmith'. The ironsmith is a master of his profession, renowned among peers and public alike for the beauty of his work. He has trained many apprentice ironsmiths who have gone on to develop similar mastery. The ironsmith knows nothing of the molecular structure of iron, nor does he conceive of such a theory, but he knows a good piece of iron!*

> He also knows how to heat and hit iron into shape, and yet he knows nothing
> of what he does to the iron or why the intervention is successful. Similarly, his
> apprentices watch and learn the technique, developing mastery of their craft, but
> cannot express their skill in any verbal or written form.

The history of the health professions has been dominated by such apprenticeship-type learning. Clinical problems have been solved by a whole array of strategies, often without a clear understanding of why or how these strategies were successful. The practitioner learns to solve similar problems in similar ways — intervention is determined by a knowledge of past results modified to meet new situations through the comparison of present feedback with that of the past. Knowledge becomes embodied or tacit and is expressed as an intuitive skill of the craftsman. While this may produce highly skilled practitioners, they will not have the ability to make their knowledge explicit (like the ironsmith in the example above) and if reasoning cannot be questioned, it cannot be understood. Without explicit reasoning, there is a 'watch and learn' approach to therapy, which restricts professional development (of the individual and the profession) to inductive practice — it fails to enable a deductive approach, where new treatment can be generated based on the prevailing theoretical understanding.

What is clinical reasoning?

Clinical reasoning is commonly defined in terms of clinical problem solving. For example, Carr (2004) refers to it as the process of applying knowledge and expertise to a clinical situation to develop a solution. However, Higgs *et al* (2004) offer a simple definition that embraces contexts of practice beyond the purely clinical:

> *The thinking and decision-making processes which occur in professional practice.*
> (Higgs *et al*, 2004, p182)

Reasoning is an essential feature of professional practice — it sets autonomous professionals apart from technicians (who are instructed by decision-makers). Furthermore, the reasoning behind clinical interventions is the fundamental basis for professional clinical efficacy. Where reasoning is absent, interventions enter the realm of guesswork and become habit (at best) or whim and fancy (at worst). Professionals are better able to make their decision-making processes explicit where the process and content of clinical reasoning are clear.

Numerous models of clinical reasoning exist, and all seek to enable the practitioner to better explicate practice (for examples, see Higgs *et al*, 2008; Fleming and Mattingly, 2008; Banning, 2008). While they are not all covered here, any process by which reasoning is made explicit, or assumed knowledge is tested, can be utilised as a tool for CPD using the approach described below. The process of cognitive mapping is offered as a model by which reasoning processes can be translated into meaningful CPD.

Cognitive mapping

Higgs (1992a,b, 1993) developed the concept of cognitive mapping, which enables the practitioner to take a clinical episode and identify the theoretical and practical knowledge, skills and evidence that can be considered (and used) when attempting to implement an effective therapeutic strategy. It is perhaps easiest to follow this type of reasoning through a series of examples.

Figure 7.1 illustrates a simple mathematical problem — if we know the height of the lighthouse (AC) and the distance from the top of the lighthouse to the ship (AB), then how far is the ship from the base of the lighthouse (BC)? To successfully solve this problem, the 'practitioner' uses several schema of knowledge, all of which contribute to an understanding of Pythagoras' theorem. *Figure 7.2* maps some of the component schema that must be understood

Figure 7.1. A simple mathematical problem Recognising a right-angled triangle, we can apply Pythagoras' theorem to determine the length of any 'side', providing we know the length of the other two 'sides'.

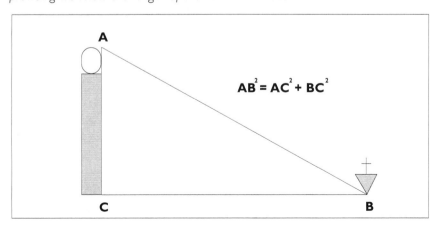

$$AB^2 = AC^2 + BC^2$$

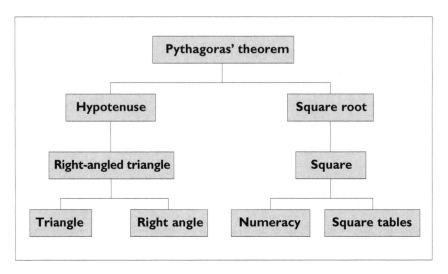

Figure 7.2. Mapping the conceptual schema used to understand Pythagoras' theorem.

to comprehend this theorem, including basic numeracy and the concepts of 'triangle', 'right angle', 'hypotenuse' and 'square root'. Some schema are sub-concepts of others, and that these 'component schema' must first be understood in order to construct 'larger' schema. For example, to understand a 'right angle' requires an understanding of angles, degrees and some general principles of geometry. When solving a problem, practitioners have to be certain that the evidence they use to construct each schema is reliable and valid. They must also recognise that schema have to be related and assimilated in order to solve the problem — unless all the concepts are used to inform each other, the solution will not be found. Thus, the practitioner requires cognitive skills of analysis and synthesis, and not simply declarative knowledge.

It is essential that therapists recognise the vast array of skills and areas of knowledge that are involved when considering an 'everyday' clinical problem. *Figure 7.3* considers some of the basic schema involved. The components identified are by no means exhaustive, and it should be recognised that different problems will require different areas of knowledge. Each schema can be further 'mapped' to explore all of the components within it, thus, a therapist's professional skills may include communication, teaching, management, patient handling, motivation and a whole array of therapeutic activities that will be founded on further schema. A conceptual domain such as anatomy (not

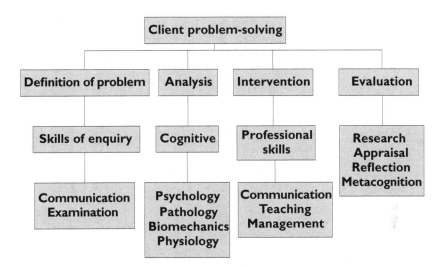

Figure 7.3. Mapping some of the basic conceptual schema used in clinical problem solving and decision-making.

identified here) would need further mapping — sub-units could be traced down a hierarchy of concepts such as joint, synovium, articulation, cartilage, collagen, chondroblasts, cellular form and function. Furthermore, each 'level' would cross-reference other domains, such as physiology, biomechanics and pathology.

Figure 7.4 (overleaf) offers a simple map to consider one clinical problem. Here, the practitioner has 'exploded' the problem 'knee pain' and started to map the component 'chunks' of knowledge that will need to be understood if the problem as a whole is to be effectively understood and addressed. By exploring clinical problems and identifying the component schema that are involved in addressing these problems, knowledge is made explicit — both what is known and what is used when carrying out 'therapy'. Hence, cognitive mapping can be used to assess both knowledge and skill bases, in relation to practice.

Together with questioning the validity and reliability of knowledge, this reflective exercise enables practitioners to see which schema should be assimilated and how different aspects of theory and practice intermesh, to form cohesive and consistent practice.

Therapists are further enabled to question their 'intuition' or 'tacit-embodied knowledge' (Higgs *et al* 2008a), by identifying exactly where each aspect of intervention originates and what 'evidence' supports these actions (including the validity of that support). However, to do this therapists require

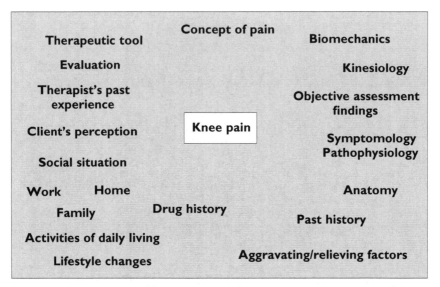

Figure 7.4. A basic map of key concepts relating to the understanding of 'knee pain'. Each of these schema can be further refined into smaller subunits, which must all be understood in order to fully understand the central concept.

'metacognition' skills (the ability to analyse and understand their own thinking and cognitive skills/processes) (Sim and Richardson, 2004). Once embodied (tacit) knowledge has been made explicit, it can be questioned; if it can be questioned, it can be understood. From this understanding comes the potential diagnosis of strengths and deficiencies in knowledge and skills. This awareness becomes the foundation for professional development (moving the individual and therefore the profession forwards).

Thus, clinical reasoning is a tool for exploring professional 'know how' — it can be used to address everything that the therapist brings to the clinical problem-solving episode, and it can help to differentiate between the source and strength of different pieces of 'evidence' that are utilised in any aspect of their role.

Elsewhere, reasoning and decision making have been explored as products of the individual practitioner's 'weighting' of multiple and inter-related pieces of 'evidence' (Stephenson, 2004), such that cognitive processes relate to the understanding and inter-relatedness of individual 'chunks' of evidence. Metacognition skills enable practitioners to recognise the context and the processes involved in 'weighting' each 'chunk'.

Developing CPD: articulating reasoning

A potential problem with any clinical reasoning tool is the implicit notion that engagement will automatically lead to enlightenment and change. A novice to clinical reasoning might carry out the activity but fail to determine whether the 'chunks' of content identified in their cognitive map are sound or weak. They could also fail to recognise that specific skills are needed, or be unaware of the knowledge or evidence base that is required. More commonly, they will lack the metacognition skills that are necessary to fully understand how their map was constructed and what should be done with it. In short, they may not be able to ascertain the relative 'weight' of each 'chunk'. In such cases, clinical reasoning may not lead to enlightenment. More likely, the *status quo* will be perpetuated, as previously successful strategies are 'weighted' highly in the absence of competing information. This is decision making by habit — the evidence used is sound and skills are clearly identified and practised with great efficiency, but as there is no recognition of other potential influences, there is no exploration that any change must occur. For these reasons, it may be beneficial to apply a mentor or peer-review process to clinical reasoning, which can test assumptions and challenge the 'weights' given to specific 'chunks'.

Role of a mentor

Consider a model wherein clinical reasoning is used as an analytical tool to identify what practitioners require to operate effectively. The tool is primarily employed by the individual, but their reasoning is made explicit to others — possibly peers, senior professionals or a mentor (an expert guide). The findings identify what therapists hold as strengths and weaknesses, based on their development to date, and indicate areas for future development, which can address their specific needs. At this point we might usefully substitute clinical reasoning for professional reasoning. Thus, this model would be highly appropriate for a professional with not only a clinical role, but somebody who also has needs based in management skills, service development, educational theory or research — such reasoning would be equally applicable to all areas.

This tool could be formalised as part of the appraisal process/individual performance review. With mentor support, the reasoning process could be applied to a series of practice-specific problems to establish the individual's specific needs (emerging themes). If these needs were then satisfied, the individual would be enabled to operate more efficiently in their professional field. As such, this process would be a means of formulating the required content and process of professional development, and would be able to identify clear objectives/goals associated with enhanced practice. It would identify specific end points and the processes that would achieve them. These end points would take different amounts of time to achieve, so there would be both short- and long-term development goals.

A learning (or development) contract could then be constructed to address the needs and aims identified, guiding the development process. Professional development activities may require monitoring and evaluation via different media, such as a reflective (professional) diary (Spalding, 2004) or portfolio (Stewart 2004).

Benefits of clinical reasoning in appraisal

There are three major benefits of such a system. First, professionals generate their own criteria for development. Professional development is highly personal, while the review process recognises ('authorises') the logic and plan used as professionally appropriate and relevant. Peer review need not mean uniprofessional — there may be benefits should other professionals use the same reasoning process. A different perspective on the reasoning employed, or on the potential application, content and 'weighting' of the identified (or non-identified) 'chunks' might generate new professional interpretations and suggest novel directions for development. It might also offer a realistic context for the development plan in terms of what is available and what can be supported in a particular environment.

Second, by not imposing a system of prescribed development (in the form of professional standards or a predetermined route), new areas of development (that were not previously part of the reasoning process) can be identified. If the logic is sound and can be justified to peers, these new developments can be pursued, leading to change. The focus is on the process of development in achieving self-directed (but professionally monitored) aims — these will often be common across many professionals of similar development, but will also include highly specific, individual direction.

Third, the process encourages reflection across an individual's lifespan as evidence, and contexts evolve to shift the weight of individual 'chunks' over time. The novice and mentor can both benefit from the process. The novice's exploration might lead experienced practitioners to question the foundations of their own understanding — reasoning is an iterative process of engagement between knowledge, cognition and metacognition, all of which have the capacity to advance over time. Equally the experienced practitioner, by making explicit the knowledge, cognitive and metacognitive processes they utilise within the reasoning episode, will support and facilitate the development of the novice.

Conclusions

CPD can be seen as a short-term or long-term activity. Development is lifelong, but there is often a desire to see immediate improvement. CPD can be self-determined, generated by autonomous professionals seeking to continually enhance their personal standards, but it is also imposed through regulatory requirements. At its worst, CPD is developed as a product-based system, pre-defining the product as a series of behaviours, or standards, that each individual must adhere to. This causes professions to move towards a predetermined, standardised, measurable and uniform state, forming a closed system that perpetuates the profession as it exists — standards are defined by what exists already and potential change is not easily incorporated. Such a system effectively restricts development and 'dwarfs' the profession. At its best, CPD can be process-based, where professionals negotiate their own specific development by declaring their needs and justifying their aims and proposed activities to their peers. This empowers the individual and offers self-direction (within reasonable, professionally-determined boundaries), with the potential to move beyond present practice. It enables innovation, creativity and originality in thought and action, taking the individual and the profession into new dimensions. This can be measured, but it requires a time-scale appropriate for change.

Potential for CPD

The potential role of clinical reasoning as a tool for CPD is vast — it can be utilised to investigate CPD and to determine individual (and possibly collective) needs. However, to establish confidence in this process, a full understanding of such reasoning and the peer-review process are paramount.

This is a tool that can be used by all professionals, irrespective of their expertise and area of practice. CPD can develop via the mastery of one tool in all professional groups. It offers a forum for multi-professional discourse and analysis of practice, with the potential for cross-fertilisation of ideas and knowledge. Most importantly, it gives meaning to CPD and ensures that vital energy is channelled into activities that the professional 'owns', rather than into the collection of specific 'CPD points' required in the next 12 months.

In the absence of an all-encompassing system that uses clinical reasoning as a tool for CPD, the above model remains highly worthwhile for individuals, departments and professional groups. It opens whole areas of the knowledge base for discussion and encourages this knowledge to be questioned and critically evaluated. By making the individual's strengths and weaknesses explicit, it can be a threat, and to this end the mentor system should explore the real depth of understanding in the individual. As a group activity, however, focusing on a specific area of common involvement provides a major facilitation to multiprofessional understanding and can be an arena for shared development.

Key points

- Clinical reasoning can be used to explicate both 'real' and hypothetical client problems across uni- or inter-professional practice
- The tool can be used individually, within peer groups or in conjunction with an experienced mentor
- By reflecting on the relative strengths and weaknesses — knowledge, cognition and metacognition — of the individual (or team) in relation to clinical reasoning, the outcomes can be used to direct CPD for the individual or team
- By utilising a common medium of analysis of practice, clinical reasoning promotes a strong and client-focused forum for multiprofessional discourse

Acknowledgements
The author would like to thank Dr Geoffery Kidd for early discussions and collaboration on the use of mapping and reasoning in developing professional understanding.

84

References

Banning M (2008) Clinical reasoning and its application to nursing: Concepts and research studies. *Nurse Education in Practice* **8**(3): 177–83

Carr S (2004) A framework for understanding clinical reasoning in community nursing. *Journal of Clinical Nursing* **13**(7): 850–7

Devlin K (1991) *Logic and information.* Cambridge University Press, Cambridge

Fleming M, Mattingly C (2008) Action and narrative: Two dynamics of clinical reasoning. In: Higgs J, Jones M, Loftus S, Christensen N eds *Clinical reasoning in the health professions.* 3rd edn. Butterworth Heinemann, Philadelphia: 55–64

Higgs J (1992a) Developing clinical reasoning competencies. *Physiotherapy* **78**(8): 575–81

Higgs J (1992b) Developing knowledge: A process of construction mapping and review. *New Zealand Journal of Physiotherapy* **20**(2): 23–30

Higgs J (1993) A programme for developing clinical reasoning skills in graduate physiotherapists. *Medical Teacher* **15**(2/3): 195–205

Higs J, Fish D, Rothwell R (2008a) Knowledge generation and clinical reasoning in practice. In: Higgs J, Jones M, Loftus S, Christensen N eds *Clinical reasoning in the health professions.* 3rd edn. Butterworth Heinemann, Philadelphia: 163–72

Higgs J, Jones M (2008) Clinical decision making and muliple problem spaces. In: Higgs J, Jones M, Loftus S, Christensen N eds *Clinical reasoning in the health professions* 3rd edn. Butterworth Heinemann, Philadelphia: 1–18

Higgs J, Jones M, Edwards I, Beeston S (2004) Clinical reasoning and practice knowledge. In: Higgs J, Richardson B, Abrandt-Dahlgren M eds *Developing practice knowledge for health professionals.* Butterworth Heinemann, Edinburgh: 181–99

Higgs J, Jones M, Loftus S, Christensen N eds (2008) *Clinical reasoning in the health professions* 3rd edn. Butterworth Heinemann, Philadelphia

Sim J, Richardson B (2004) The use and generation of practice knowledge in the context of regulating systems and moral frameworks. In: Higgs J, Richardson B, Abrandt-Dahlgren M eds. *Developing practice knowledge for health professionals.* Butterworth Heinemann, Edinburgh: 127–46

Spalding N (2004) Reflection in professional development. In: Chia S, Harrison D eds. *Tools for continuing professional cevelopment.* Quay Books, Dinton: 49–61

Stephenson R (2004) Using a complexity model of human behaviour to help interprofessional clinical reasoning. *International Journal of Therapy and Rehabilitation* **11**(4):

168–74

Stewart S (2004) The place of portfolios within continuing professional development. In: Chia S, Harrison D eds. *Tools for continuing professional development.* Quay Books, Dinton: 10–22

Chapter 8

Reflection in professional development: personal experiences

Introduction

Nicola Spalding

As indicated by the large amount of literature on the subject, the topic of reflection is immense. In the past 20 years, reflective practice has been recognised as a significant method for healthcare professionals to continue their professional development (Castle, 1996; Routledge *et al*, 1997; Stewart, 1998). Among the literature, however, there are some potentially confusing inconsistencies, with various definitions of the term 'reflection' and different accounts for the process. Rather than adding to these debates, the intention of this chapter is to demonstrate, with two case studies, how reflection has been used to improve practice. The hope is that it will clarify the process and motivate those who wish to improve their reflection skills.

What is reflection?

Donald Schön (1983) first introduced the idea of a reflective practitioner — a person who learns through personal and professional experiences. Reflection is, therefore, learning from experience.

> *Reflective practice can take place on a formal or informal basis anytime one or more persons begin a process of inquiry for the purpose of examining actions and events as a means to understand and improve performance.*
>
> (Osterman and Kottkamp, 1993)

Reflection is a process-based learning activity (Stewart, 1998), which is self-directing and thus purposeful to the learner.

Reflective skills

An informative and coherent analysis of the literature by Atkins and Murphy (1993) revealed certain cognitive and affective skills required of the reflective practitioner, namely the ability to:

- **Be self-aware** — this enables a person to honestly analyse his or her feelings
- **Be descriptive** — a comprehensive detailed account of the situation is brought to the fore from a recollection of the event and experience
- **Critically analyse** — the examination of all the elements of the situation, such as existing knowledge, assumptions and possible alternatives; the 'So what?' questions
- **Synthesise ideas** — the incorporation of previous knowledge with newly-acquired knowledge to give a new perspective on the situation
- **Evaluate** — also to give the new perspective. This is the assessment or appraisal of the situation from which judgements of worth can be made.

Schön (1991) advocates that a reflective practitioner also requires intuition. From the author's own experience, it seems possible to develop these skills while reflecting, so it is not essential that you have them all before attempting to reflect. The author has also found that certain tools, to be discussed below, enable the development and improvement of these skills.

Why reflect?

By reflecting on our past experiences we can better understand what happened, which can inform future experiences. It has been recognised for many years that reflection has the capacity to facilitate learning. Thus, reflective practice can improve professional performance, ensuring that patients receive the best possible care.

This is recognised by professional regulatory bodies, including the Health Professions Council (HPC), the Nursing and Midwifery Council (NMC) and the General Medical Council (GMC) — reflection is a recommended CPD activity, and all registrants are required to engage in CPD. The importance of reflection is evident in regulatory body standards, for example:

- The HPC requires registrants to 'understand the need for career-long self-directed learning' and 'be able to audit, reflect on and review practice' (Standards of Proficiency 2007 p4–5)

- The GMC in 'Tomorrow's Doctors' (2009) requires graduates to have established 'the foundations for lifelong learning and continuing professional development, including a professional development portfolio containing reflections, achievements and learning needs.' (p26)
- The NMC in its standards for education (2010) states that nurses must be able to 'identify one's own professional development needs by engaging in activities such as reflection in, and on, practice and lifelong learning' (p34).

Registered health professionals are required to provide evidence of CPD, so it is important that healthcare students learn to document reflection as well as practice it. Pre-registration curricula have been designed to help students develop, practice and document reflective skills in the classroom and in practice settings. Thus, all newly qualified health professionals have reflection experience and skills for continuing reflective practice throughout their careers.

Two personal experiences are presented below, to illustrate the stages in the process of reflection and how they can serve both learning and practice.

Personal experience I

Earlier in my lecturing career I recognised a personal need to develop and improve my teaching skills. I wanted to equip myself with what I perceived I lacked, in terms of practice and theory, as a result of not having a teaching qualification when I first started lecturing.

> *Learning to teach involves the development of technical skills as well as an appreciation of moral issues involved in education, an ability to negotiate and develop one's practice within the culture of the school, and an ability to reflect and evaluate in and on one's actions.*

(Calderhead, 1991, p531)

Schön (1991) suggests that reflection is most likely initiated when a professional is dissatisfied with his or her performance. I therefore decided to carry out an evaluation of my abilities and make improvements in light of the evaluation. This is the first stage in the reflective process, which Boyd and Fales (1983) refer to as 'a sense of inner discomfort'. For me it was the impetus for self-evaluation and improvement.

Another tool to help identify learning goals might result from a personal 'strengths, weaknesses, opportunities and threats' (SWOT) analysis (Atkinson, 1998). My learning opportunities were my teaching sessions.

The second stage of the reflective process is one of information-gathering and critical analysis. This is an examination of feelings and knowledge, which is seen as constructive development. To evaluate myself, I filmed some of my teaching sessions so that I could subsequently watch myself teaching. I also kept a reflective diary, which required me to document my experiences — I used this diary after every lesson in which I taught. Thorpe (1993) suggests that writing is a way of capturing thoughts and feelings and of structuring and using reflection strategically for intentional learning.

First, I described the practice situation. Second, to analyse the experience I answered the following questions:

- What did I feel both during and after the situation?
- What was positive about the situation and why?
- What felt less positive and why?
- What were my reasons for my practice?
- In light of this analysis, what would I do differently next time?
- What did I learn from the situation?

I discussed the situation with colleagues, documenting their responses and suggestions and my thoughts on what they said — thus a range of perspectives were considered (Fish *et al*, 1991).

The filmed sessions were all viewed and written up in the same way. To encourage the analytical process it is important to justify actions and consider their theoretical basis, so I stated reasons for my behaviour. I was then able to refer to the literature on teaching to increase my theoretical knowledge and consider ideas and theories to improve my practice.

When descriptive data have been gathered, analysis must then be encouraged. Fish *et al* (1991, p27) state that this is:

...concerned with discovering and exploring the assumptions, beliefs and value judgments that underlie the events and the ideas which emerge...and does not merely involve superficial criticism of what happened in practice.

Of the whole reflective process, I found the most useful question to be 'In light of this analysis, what would I do differently next time?', as it moved me forwards. To give an example, one of my critical incidents was a teaching session on 'wheelchair prescription', which was held in a cramped room. In my diary, I noted that the cramped conditions had compromised safety and limited the use of audiovisual aids. At the same time, I had felt disappointed by the lack of student participation in the various activities that were incorporated into the lesson. My conclusion was that in this instance, the room I had used was obviously too small — I had only chosen it as the room had been used previously by another lecturer. I considered the poor student interactions and thought that a larger room that enabled the students to sit in a circle would facilitate better discussions. This was reinforced by the literature, which advocated a circle for encouraging student participation (Locke and Ciechalski, 1995).

Having answered the analysis question, I then planned a repeat lesson as though I was going to immediately teach it again. For the example given here, this included booking a different, larger room, considering the equipment that I wanted to use and including the circled seating arrangement on my lesson plan. Keeping a record of all these events enabled me to focus my ideas for improvement. The following year, when planning my timetable, I was able to apply the reflections from my diary. Alsop (1995) argues the importance of systematic documentation for ease of clarification and future reference.

Having performed the analysis, I was able to realise my learning — in this case, the significance of seating arrangements, the incorporation of teaching aids and the importance of planning accordingly. This is the final stage in the reflective process, the learning or outcome of reflection. Boud *et al* (1985) see this as resulting in affective and cognitive changes (the changed perspective), which may lead to behavioural changes.

The descriptive diary entries offered a large amount of material to reflect on, which made apparent just how much had happened during each session. I believe that had it not been documented, some of this information would have been forgotten and, therefore, would not have been used for reflection. I found that recording the experience in a written form stimulated my memory, enabling me to reflect in more detail than I would have been able to otherwise.

Answering the list of analytical questions gave the process structure and kept me focused. I found these questions useful as they broke each task into stages and reminded me to analyse and to move forwards. With practice, my analytical skills developed. As with any new skill, it takes practice to refine reflection.

Personal experience 2

There are recognised benefits to practising reflection in a group, with group members able to support each other and promote better understanding than might be achieved alone (Barnett, 1994). My second personal experience provides evidence of the value of group reflection.

As part of a multidisciplinary team of health professionals, I was involved in an action research project, which aimed to improve the preoperative education programme provided to patients who were awaiting total hip replacement. This research, which formed part of a large case study, was a learning opportunity for all of the health professionals involved. We had not previously met to discuss the service or evaluate its effectiveness.

Data were collected by various means, which included patient questionnaires, patient interviews, interviews with health professionals and written reflections (using the same analysis questions listed in *personal experience 1*). As part of the action research process, team meetings were held to discuss these evaluative data. Group reflections were seen to evolve in these meetings, as individuals worked together — they would ask each other questions and then debate issues that arose, thus encouraging critical analysis.

As one health professional stated:

Discussion could take place on what we were doing well and what could be improved upon.

These meetings were a place for us to legitimately reflect with the purpose of improving, and this reflection enabled us to work together for a shared purpose — something the service had previously lacked. The meetings also provided a platform for constructive feedback between health professionals and gave us the opportunity to advance previous, individual reflections on the service.

In the words of one team member:

It gave us time to think more about what we were doing to plan for the next one. I would have reflected, but not probably as much...and you hear what others have to say too, which makes you think more.

As a consequence of these reflections and discussions, the health professionals involved learned a great deal about the preoperative educational product and the preoperative educational process. They had a changed perspective, which resulted in 21 direct changes to the programme. These changes were considered to be substantial service improvements.

Overcoming hindrances to reflection

Many health professionals have increasingly heavy workloads, and reflection can be time-consuming. When compared with other duties, reflection is often judged to be of low priority, so it can be neglected. However, in the author's experience reflection improves practice a great deal, so it is worth investing time in. Furthermore, it is a recognised CPD activity, considered to be crucial in assuring the best possible care for patients. The College of Occupational Therapists (2002, p198) states that:

> *Occupational therapy personnel have a responsibility to use new technologies and new learning in order to maximize their impact for the benefit of service users and their carers.*

What to reflect on?

In the author's experience, having facilitated reflection workshops and MSc teaching, health professionals often find it difficult to choose situations to reflect on. There is a tendency to select negative experiences, which is understandable given that everybody will want to avoid repeating these — particularly if they perceive that a patient's situation could have been improved. Reflecting on negative experiences provides an excellent opportunity to review events and analyse, synthesise and evaluate what happened, with the intention of learning from the review, avoiding repeat errors and identifying learning needs, to improve skills and understanding. For the same reasons, very positive experiences have exactly the same learning potential — through reflection we can gain a better understanding of why things went well, with the intention of making sure that we repeat them.

While routine situations are not always perceived to be good opportunities for reflection (nor an easy option for analysis, as they tend to be automatic/ intuitive) their investigation often brings about a new perspective. Reflecting on everyday experiences can enable health professionals to improve their understanding and therefore their standard of care. This might be particularly important for very experienced professionals, giving them the opportunity to review their clinical reasoning and review the evidence base.

Methods of reflection

The first personal experience described above reported on several methods for stimulating reflection. It can be a solitary experience, such as the use of a written account or a film or recording, or it can be participatory and involve verbalising events with others. An experienced other can act as a mentor to encourage the reflective process by asking the questions and ensuring there is an answer. As Plato stated:

> *A wise man learns from experience, and an even wiser man from the experience of others.*

The second personal experience demonstrates how a group can reflect on an event together, with the shared purpose of improving practice.

There are also other methods. Posters, for instance, can be used to stimulate reflection. In the author's office, there is a cartoon image of various figures on a large tree. Some sit on the high branches, happy to be near the top, while others near the top look uncertain or nervous (one figure is clutching the trunk for dear life and another swings precariously from a branch). On the lower branches, there are more figures — some appear to be content with their position and some are aiming to climb higher. Some of the figures look daunted by the journey ahead. This image is by my office door and it serves as a reminder on exit to think about the day's work and where I would place myself and why, thus starting the reflective process. I have also used Robert Frost's poem, *The Road Not Taken* (1915) to think about what might or might not have been. For example, I sometimes find it helpful to think of what might have happened if I had tried a different approach to teaching. The point here is that anything can be used to stimulate reflections.

Other methods documented in the literature include:

- A reading group (Cave and Clandinin, 2007)
- Blogs (Bodell *et al*, 2009)
- 'Film and facilitated small group discussion as a means of introducing narrative reflective practice' (Brett-MacLean *et al*, 2010, p499)

- Online reflections, composed as a letter to a critical friend
- 'Making reflection public seems to have had a positive impact on the quality and style of reflection and interactions' (Rocco, 2010)
- Art (Cheng, 2010)
- Photography (Wald *et al*, 2010).

The final factor to consider is that of motivation. Being motivated to reflect on experiences will help engagement when time is very limited. This can be achieved in part by understanding the reasons for reflecting, i.e. the belief in improvement. Motivation can come from the learning that results from reflection — this encourages continuation of the process. One should acknowledge the rewards as they arise.

Conclusions

Reflection can be daunting at first. However, on closer review, the skills that are necessary for reflective practice are evident in normal daily practice. These skills are fundamental to health professionals and will have been introduced and developed during professional education.

Most practitioners regularly evaluate interventions and interactions with clients and colleagues. An obvious example is changing an intervention if no improvement is noted — to do this, the practitioner must have engaged in the reflective process, to some extent. However, for true reflective practice to take place, there must be learning that informs future practice.

As previously mentioned, there are various requirements for health professionals to document their reflections and subsequent learning. This can be necessary for the purposes of supervision, mentoring, personal development plans or appraisal interviews. Extracts from a reflective diary may be used as such evidence. For some health professionals, the shift from normal, everyday practice to reflective practice may simply be one of documenting their subsequent learning.

It is hoped that the personal experiences presented in this chapter will be of use to those who are not familiar with reflection and its process, as similar (or indeed the same) methods can be widely used. There is no prescription as to which specific tools should be used, as the best choice is always that which practitioners feel aids them to reflect on their own practice situation. However, diaries, illustrations, a set of questions, a mentor and/or a group of supportive colleagues may all be helpful. Commitment to learning the art of reflection will be rewarded, as reflective practice maximises the learning potential of many practice situations and thus aids one's CPD. This should result in high quality patient care.

Key points

- Reflective practice has been recognised for its potential in CPD
- Reflection is a process-based learning activity, which is self-directing and thus purposeful to the learner
- The reflective practitioner is required to be self-aware, descriptive, analytical, evaluative and able to synthesise ideas
- Three stages can be identified in the reflection process, namely:
  - the impetus for change
  - the critical analysis
  - the learning outcome
- Personal strategies can be used to aid the reflection process, for example illustrations and questions
- There are barriers with the potential to hinder the reflection process, so a further challenge exists to overcome them
- The final factor to consider is that of motivation. Being motivated will help commitment. This can be achieved in part by understanding the reasons for reflecting, i.e. the belief in improvement
- Documentation of learning as a consequence of reflection may be used as evidence of CPD

References

Alsop A (1995) The professional portfolio — purpose, process and practice. Part 2: producing a portfolio from experiential learning. *British Journal of Occupational Therapy* **58**(8): 337–40

Atkins S, Murphy K (1993) Reflection: a review of the literature. *Journal of Advanced Nursing* **18**(8): 1188–92

Atkinson K (1998) SWOT analysis: A tool for continuing professional development. *British Journal of Therapy and Rehabilitation* **5**(8): 433–5

Barnett R (1994) *The limits of competence: Knowledge, higher education and society.* Society for Research into Higher Education and Open University Press, Buckingham

Boud D, Keogh R, Walker D (1985) *Reflection: Turning experience into learning.* Kogan

Page, London

Bodell S, Hook A, Penman M, Wade W (2009) Creating a learning community in today's world: How blogging can facilitate continuing professional development and international learning. *British Journal of Occupational Therapy* **72**(6): 279–81

Boyd E, Fales A (1983) Reflective learning: Key to learning from experience. *Journal of Human Psychology* **23**(2): 99–117

Brett-MacLean PJ, Cave MT, Yiu V, Kelner D, Ross DJ (2010) Film as a means to introduce narrative reflective practice in medicine and dentistry: A beginning story presented in three parts'. *Reflective Practice* **11**(4): 499–516

Calderhead J (1991) The nature and growth of knowledge in student teaching. *Teaching and Teacher Education* **7**(5): 531–5

Castle A (1996) Developing the ethos of reflective practice for continuing professional development. *British Journal of Therapy and Rehabilitation* **3**(7): 358–9

Cave MT, Clandinin DJ (2007) Learning to live with being a physician. *Reflective Practice* **8**: 75–91

Cheng IK (2010) Transforming practice: Reflections on the use of art to develop professional knowledge and reflective practice. *Reflective Practice* **11**(4): 489–98

College of Occupational Therapists (2002) College of Occupational Therapists: Position statement on lifelong learning. *British Journal of Occupational Therapy* **65**(5): 198–200

Fish D, Twinn S, Purr B (1991) Promoting reflection: Improving the supervision of practice in health visiting and initial teacher training. In: *How to Enable Students to Learn Through Professional Practice*. Report 2. West London Institute of Higher Education, Middlesex

Frost R (1915) *The road not taken in Rhys Jones* (1996) The Nation's Favourite Poems BBC Books

GMC (2009) *Tomorrow's doctors.* GMC, London

HPC (2007) *Standards of proficiency.* Available from: www.hpc-uk.org

Locke D, Ciechalski C (1995) *Psychological techniques for teachers.* 2nd edn. Accelerated Development, Washington DC

NMC (2010) *Standards of proficency for preregistration nursing education.* NMC, London

Osterman K, Kottkamp R (1993) *Reflective practice for educators: Improving schooling through professional development.* Corwin Press, California

Rocco S (2010) Making reflection public: Using interactive online discussion board to enhance student learning. *Reflective Practice* **11**(3): 307–17

Routledge J, Willson M, McArthur M, Richardson B, Stephenson R (1997) Reflection on the development of a reflective assessment. *Medical Teacher* **19**(2): 122–8

Schön D (1983) *The reflective practitioner: How professionals think in action.* Basic Books, New York

Schön D (1991) *The reflective practitioner: How professionals think in action.* 2nd edn. Jossey Bass, San Francisco

Stewart S (1998) The place of portfolios within continuing professional development. *British Journal of Therapy and Rehabilitation* **5**(5): 266–9

Thorpe M (1993) Experiential learning at a distance. In: Boud D, Cohen R, Walker D, eds. *Using experience for learning.* Society for Research in Higher Education and Open University Press, Buckingham

Wald H, Norman D, Walker J (2010) Reflection through the arts: Focus on photography to foster reflection in a health care context. Living beyond - an interactive photographic exhibit. *Reflective Practice* **11**(4): 545–63

Chapter 9

Journal clubs: a tool for CPD activity

Introduction

Toby O Smith

An important aspect of evidence-based practice is to keep abreast of recent publications in key scientific journals. While all health professionals should be reading, given the plethora of available literature and the time pressures placed on practitioners, this does not always happen. The journal club is one strategy for enabling people working in health and social care to process clinically relevant research publications in a focused, meaningful and time-limited way. The purpose of this chapter is to provide an introduction to journal clubs as a continuing professional development (CPD) activity, and to provide guidance on how to establish and run such sessions.

What is a journal club?

A journal club is where a group of practitioners meets regularly to present, appraise and discuss one or more articles to inform clinical practice and professional development (Bury and Jerosch-Herold, 1998). They have been used as a means of disseminating research in medical practice for many years, with early proponents being Sir James Paget (at St Bartholomew's Hospital, London during the mid-1800s) and Sir William Osler (at McGill University, Montreal in 1875) (Paget, 1901; Linzer, 1987). However journal clubs are less common in allied health professions. A survey of 300 healthcare institutions indicated that two-fifths of UK and one-fifth of Australian physiotherapy departments ran such sessions (Turner and Mjolne, 2001).

The purpose of journal clubs

The purpose of journal clubs is three-fold:

- First, they provide an opportunity for the discussion and dissemination of literature, to inform clinical and professional practice. Practitioners are able

99

to explore up-to-date clinical issues, share and present ideas, consider different perspectives and ultimately use the discussed literature to inform departmental policy, or to validate existing practices (Taylor, 2000; Milbrandt and Vincent, 2004).

- Second, they provide an opportunity to practise the critical appraisal skills that inform evidence-based practice. Practitioners are able to develop and refine their knowledge of research methodology and analytical enquiry to inform evidence-based practice (Straus *et al*, 2005).
- Third, practitioners are enabled to demonstrate their CPD. This is imperative given that allied health professionals must demonstrate their professional development for re-registration (Health Professions Council, 2009).

Planning a journal club

When planning a journal club, a number of factors should be considered. These are discussed below:

Establishing rules

When first devising a journal club, it is sensible to establish a number of rules. These may include:

- Punctual attendance at meetings
- Respecting the comments made by other members of the group
- Confidentiality during sessions
- Equal contributions to group discussion and tasks
- Undertaking agreed plans and roles, when delegated
- Being constructive when giving feedback, in order to facilitate a supported learning environment.

It should be a firm rule that all members read the article prior to the meeting. This is to ensure that precious 'discussion' and 'analysis' time in the meeting is not lost. Furthermore, if reading is rushed, there will not be sufficient time to reflect on and analyse the article, so only superficial discussion may be generated.

Environment

Consideration should be given to the room in which the group meets. Journal clubs are mostly run in an informal group setting, allowing each member to face one another to facilitate discussion. Accordingly one means of promoting interaction to stimulate debate is to arrange chairs in a circle to make the environment appear less threatening than a formal classroom layout.

Timing and duration of sessions

It has been recommended that the timing and frequency of journal club meetings be standardised (Morton, 1996; Cutcliffe and Ward, 2007). To maximise attendance, sessions are usually run at times that are more convenient for busy clinicians. Some groups meet at lunchtimes, reasoning that more practitioners are likely to attend and that clinical practice will not be interrupted (Esdaile and Roth, 2004). However, this means that sessions are always time-constrained, which potentially curtails extended discussion. Esdaile and Roth (2004) suggest meeting over a number of lunchtimes in a specific week, or holding a longer session once a week to allow sufficient time to fully explore an article without the discussion losing momentum. Some practitioners run clubs during a designated morning or afternoon each month. When organised in this way, sessions can be routinely planned around clinical practice and provide ample time for extended discussion.

The frequency of meetings may be determined by clinical practicalities, the depth of discussion, members' learning needs and/or the size of topics covered. Provided the journal club remains a workable and beneficial resource, the duration and frequency of meetings should be immaterial.

Size of group

It has been recommended that the size of each journal club should be between two and 10 practitioners (Taylor, 2004). The benefits of learning in a group are outlined by Straus *et al* (2005) as follows:

- It can facilitate discussion of broader questions about a topic
- Multiple viewpoints are available to interpret answers

- Experienced and less experienced members of a group can be paired up for specific tasks
- Groups offer 'peer support' so that members can provide feedback to each other as a 'reality check' to an individual's perception of his or her learning level
- Groups provide camaraderie and interpersonal support to make learning more fun than it would be in isolation
- It can facilitate the sharing out of roles, work and responsibility so the onus of maintaining the club does not fall on a small number of individuals
- Once members have gained confidence in their searching and appraisal methods, multiple publications can be reviewed over a series of meetings. This can enable clubs to generate consensus statements on specific topics to inform departmental policy and professional practice.

Groups of more than 10–12 practitioners may be too large for all members to have the opportunity to present their viewpoint and interact in discussions, particularly during sessions of less than an hour.

Identification of members' strengths and weaknesses

Before joining a journal club, it is important to ask members to reflect on their strengths and weaknesses. The reasons for this are two-fold. First, it is important that members' prior knowledge of a particular research methodology or clinical area is known to the group, as such, individuals can be a resource, to facilitate peer-support and share important knowledge for the group's benefit. Second, by identifying members' weaknesses, such areas can be specifically addressed to develop the group's research knowledge, or clinical awareness, thereby developing evidence-based practice as part of CPD. Through regular reflection, such weaknesses can be redefined as goals, thereby nurturing CPD and the evolution of the journal club.

Pre-teaching

Before the group ventures to critically appraise its first article, journal club organisers may consider arranging some 'pre-teaching' sessions. This is important to develop the group's basic understanding of research methodology. These may be particularly useful where there is a broad spectrum of prior research experience. Didactic teaching sessions may include topics such as:

* Methods of identifying literature
* Interpretation of results
* Principles of statistical tests
* Appraisal methods for different research designs (Carley *et al*, 1998).

If this teaching is provided, all members will have a baseline level of knowledge required to engage in meaningful critical appraisal.

Single vs. multiple paper meetings

There are merits to discussing single papers during journal club meetings and merits to discussing several. Taylor (2004) recommends that a single article should be discussed when starting a journal club, to enable members to develop their appraisal skills before tackling multiple papers. When this commonality of critical appraisal knowledge is established, multiple publications may then be reviewed during each meeting, to broaden the group's discussion. The appraisal of multiple articles can offer divergent views, potentially leading to more interesting discussions during each meeting (Taylor, 2000; 2004). The choice to discuss single or multiple papers is based on the time available for each session, the size of the evidence base for a specific topic, and the appraisal skills of a club's membership.

Re-evaluation

At its inception, the group should plan regular times to formally reflect on its progress. This can be used to assess the success to which the group have met their original objectives. These objectives may relate to how well the group has developed its knowledge of the available clinical evidence, how well it has refined or developed its members' skills in literature searching, critical appraisal methods, presentation and group discussion, and how these have enhanced members' CPD. Such reflection will allow for the cultivation and redefining of the group's learning objectives, to ensure that it meets the evolving needs of its members.

Journal club members

Journal clubs can be uniprofessional or multidisciplinary, depending on the setting and the topics discussed (Taylor, 2004). If articles are not relevant, interesting or professionally useful to members, then clubs are doomed to fail. It can be difficult to find articles that are relevant to every member. This may have a detrimental effect on the attraction of some members toward meetings. For example, an article about the rehabilitation of neurologically impaired individuals may be of interest to allied health professionals, nurses, doctors and managers involved in the care of these patients, but it may be of little interest to those with limited contact with this patient group. To include members of different disciplines has advantages, such as broadening the range of viewpoints during discussion. In addition, if the journal club intends to devise clinical policy, it can be advantageous to include professionals of all disciplines that may be affected (Sherratt, 2005). However, to include members from many different professions may reduce the depth to which a group can discuss profession-specific topics. There may also be greater logistical difficulties when organising a multi-professional group, as managers, workloads and working practices differ across professions (Sherratt, 2005). Finally, it is extremely important that all members of the group feel sufficiently comfortable presenting to the group, and are able to discuss topics to the level they wish without feeling dominated or threatened by other members from different professions. In some multidisciplinary groups this may be an issue.

Joining a journal club is a commitment, and membership should be voluntary. Members who are cajoled or forced into participating may consider meetings a chore rather than a useful CPD activity (Sheehan, 1994) and this can be reflected in dwindling attendance and poor compliance to the roles and responsibilities of club membership.

In every club, there are several key roles that need to be allocated, and each of these can be viewed as time-consuming and onerous (Taylor, 2004). To prevent this feeling developing, these roles can be rotated among members. Larger journal clubs can allocate tasks jointly to two or three people, which enables more experienced members to teach skills and provide advice to less experienced or less confident members (Straus *et al*, 2005).

Specific roles within a journal club are listed below.

Chair

The group should be lead by a Chair, who should ensure that each meeting addresses the club's key objectives:
*   To critically appraise the article presented
*   To assess its clinical relevance
*   To ask members to consider whether the article's findings should be introduced in their practice.

The Chair may be responsible for explaining specific clinical or methodological jargon, to ensure that each member of the group understands the technical issues under discussion. Accordingly, to ensure that the most suitably qualified member is in a position to advise his or her colleagues, the Chair may rotate according to the topic of the paper being presented. The Chair is also responsible for addressing any group dynamic issues which may impede learning. These can include a dominating over-participator, or a quiet non-participator (Straus *et al*, 2005).

At the end of each session, the Chair must summarise what has happened, so that each member understands the key 'take home message'. They must also collaborate with the group to devise a research or CPD question to be discussed during the next meeting.

Article searcher

One member should be responsible for identifying and obtaining the article for discussion based on the research question posed by the group. This role is therefore dependent on the individual's ability to identify pertinent literature, and then to obtain and distribute copies of this to the members. It may be prudent, particularly in the early stages, to seek assistance from a medical librarian to ensure that the most appropriate articles are sourced. This role has been made easier with the popularisation of open-access publications, allowing greater availability of academic articles for review (Allebeck, 2006). Once an article is identified, the 'article searcher' can either send an electronic link for each member to individually access the article, or photocopy and distribute the article by hand, bearing in mind copyright restrictions. This should be sent a minimum of 7 days before the meeting, to allow members sufficient time to read and reflect on the article. The 'article searcher' may also be responsible for providing copies of the journal club checklist, so that members can begin to critique the article before the club meets.

Critical appraisal expert

Cutcliffe and Ward (2007) suggested it is beneficial for someone experienced in critiquing research to lead the appraisal section of the meeting. Partnerships between academics and practitioners can be a favourable experience in developing and nurturing a journal club (Austin and Richter, 2009). This may be particularly important given that occupational therapists, for example, find it difficult to interpret scientific literature (Dubouloz *et al*, 1999). However, such opportunities may not exist for all journal clubs. Nevertheless, gaining technical advice on critical appraisal methods may be of considerable benefit, particularly during the conception of the journal club.

Refreshments provider

Journal clubs have a social importance. They can provide a forum for practitioners to meet and discuss clinical problems and relate these to the evidence-base. It has been recommended that such discussion can be accompanied by food, particularly when meetings are held over lunchtimes or after work (Esdaile and Roth, 2004; Deenadayalan *et al*, 2008). Accordingly, someone should be responsible for co-ordinating refreshments to give a social perspective to this CPD activity. When the costs involved in providing lunch are too high, members can bring their own lunch, so that they can eat during the meeting.

Minute taker

In some cases it may be advisable for one member to take notes on proceedings. This is an optional role, as it may be that all members complete their own records to incorporate into their CPD portfolio. However, for groups devising departmental policy, a secretary to take important notes on clinical planning can be advantageous, to ensure that the discussion during a meeting is accurately reflected in subsequent decisions made.

Selection of articles

Once the journal club has been planned, the roles of its members defined, and a research question chosen by the group, it is then the responsibility of the 'article searcher' to select the published work to meet this research question. The decision on what literature should be chosen may be based on the objectives of the journal club, and its learning needs. Straus *et al* (2005) categorised such learning needs into three possibilities:

- **Needs-driven** — topics are selected which have clinical equipoise requiring a decision to gain consensus. For example, an article, or series of articles may be selected to inform the management of a specific patient being treated by a member of the group at the time of the meeting
- **Evidence-driven** — literature is selected which has uncertainty within the evidence-base. For example, the journal club may select an article to allow members to comment on contemporary issues raised by the Department of Health, a professional body, or, at a local level, by hospital management policy
- **Skills-driven** — literature is selected which will facilitate members' learning of specific skills of research methods or appraisal techniques. For example, an article reporting a randomised controlled trial may be selected to allow members an opportunity to critique this design to develop their knowledge of this research approach.

The selection of literature for discussion should be driven by patients' or learners' needs, rather than the activities of publishers, distributors, researchers or editors (Straus *et al*, 2005). Accordingly, consultation with a medical librarian is suggested as one means of ensuring that journal clubs can 'hunt out' pertinent literature to answer their research or CPD questions, rather than being restricted by publication bias or issues of access and availability.

Format of a journal club

Outlining the research question

The first stage of each journal club session should be spent reminding each member of the previously agreed research question. The Chair can use this opportunity to outline the plan for the meeting and keep the group focused on answering this question.

Reflection on the paper

Although it is recommended that all the members of the group should have read the article before the meeting, the Chair may feel it prudent to allow some time for members to refresh themselves with the article, or for those who have forgotten to read the paper, to do so. Whilst this may only be for a couple minutes, it allows members to collect their thoughts on how the article relates to the agreed research question, and will also give late-comers time to arrive before the discussion begins.

Presenting the paper

Historically, journal clubs have been led by one person who presents his or her chosen article and discusses its methodology and clinical relevance during a 10 to 15 minute synopsis, following which it is opened up to the group for discussion (Mensch and Mitchell, 2003). This mode of journal club has become outdated, with encouragement for group appraisal and discussion, rather than the onus being on one presenter (Straus *et al*, 2005). By opening the discussion to the entire group, the members are able to engage with all articles, re-enforcing each member's critical appraisal and presentation skills, whilst gaining attitudes from different viewpoints.

Straus *et al* (2005) and Taylor (2004) recommend that the discussion of a paper should be based on an appraisal checklist to structure the proceedings. Factors to present and discuss may include: the objectives of the article, study setting, research design, population, outcome tools used, measurement periods, interventions, results, statistical analysis, and clinical application. Similarly, specific tools may be adopted as guidelines for critical appraisal. Tools such as the PEDro score (Maher *et al*, 2003), the CASP tool (PHRU, 2007), or the AGREE tool (AGREE, 2001) may act as a structure, particularly for novice researchers. The use of a structured checklist also ensures that both the article's critical appraisal points and the clinical implications are considered, whilst future learning needs are identified, which may be missed if not presented in such a structured fashion. It also removes some pressure from the Chair to ensure that each of these areas is addressed during the meeting. The checklist can also be used to document a member's learning, as it can be incorporated into the member's portfolio, to demonstrate CPD activity. An example of a checklist is presented in *Table 9.1.*

Table 9.1. Journal Club Checklist

Date: 1st April 2011
Article reviewed: Lambeek *et al* (2010) Randomised controlled trial of integrated care to reduce disability from chronic low back pain in working and private life. *BMJ* 340: 1035.
Chair-person: Chia Swee Hong
Article searcher: Toby Smith

Paper's rationale for study:
Low back pain is a major problem that is associated with chronic pain and disability. Little research has been undertaken on preventing exacerbations of low back pain in the workplace. The authors developed an integrated service using a bio-psycho-social model of management for those working with chronic low back pain. This paper reports the 12-month results of this novel service.

Summary of study: (population, interventions, outcomes, follow-up periods, results)
134 adults who had been off sick due to low back pain for a minimum of 12 weeks; 68 randomised to usual care, 66 to the new integrated care. Integrated care included a workplace ergonomics assessment, and a graded activity programme using cognitive-behaviour therapy principles. Treatment was administered over 12 weeks, involving an occupational physician, occupational therapist, and physiotherapist working with subjects and their workplace supervisors. Usual care was the usual treatment provided by their general practitioner, occupational physician and/or allied health professional. Subjects were followed-up over 12 months. Results indicated a significantly shorter duration of reduced working activities, with higher functional outcomes at 12 months. No difference in pain score.

Critical appraisal comments made:
Power calculation adopted and the study was sufficiently large. Appropriate outcome measures to the research question, with long enough follow-up period. Clear and well-conducted randomisation process, with appropriate stratification. No blinding of assessors but this was discussed within paper. Subject flow clearly demonstrated. Was there a difference in days off work between the groups at baseline – did this affect the results?

Reflection:
Has this paper developed my critical appraisal skills?

Table 9.1 cont/

Table 9.1. Journal Club Checklist (cont/)

This paper gave me the opportunity to learn about the importance of a power calculation. Through further reading and discussion in the group, I have learnt how this is constructed, what it means in respect to statistical error, and the importance of basing the sample size on this calculation. I also learnt about stratification of patients at the time of randomisation to ensure equal numbers of patients in each group for important characteristics.

Was this paper clinically relevant to me, and how?
This paper has limited direct clinical relevance to me currently as I don't work in this environment.

How can this paper be applied to my patients?
...However, the paper has indicated that cognitive-behavioural therapy and graded activity may be useful in the treatment of patients with low back pain who are returning to work. This is a group of patients who I occasionally treat. I will investigate further these two treatment approaches in my reading.

How does this paper sit in my understanding of this topic in relation to other evidence?
This was the first paper I have read specifically using such an integrated treatment approach with this patient group. I have read about the usefulness of cognitive-behavioural therapy and graded activities with other patients, and the same beneficial results have been previously reported. This therefore provides further support for these two treatments.

Should this paper change my clinical practice, and how?
Currently no. I need to look at the use of this pathway for patients treated in my clinical setting. I am not sure how much effect the improved communication with the patient's supervisor had alone, as we would have less contact with firms than this in our practice.

Do we need to further assess this topic in another club session, or with future research?
Further assessment of such pathways in other clinical areas would be beneficial. Further knowledge on survival analysis graphs would be helpful as Figure 2 confused me.

What is the take-home message?
Integrated pathways for low back pain may help patients return to work. Their use in clinical practice is less clear. Power calculations are very important in being able to answer a research question.

In the main, groups often work through a selected article with discussion and debate. However, techniques such as flip-chart mind-mapping sessions, or role-play can act as useful adjuncts to supplement group discussion when considering methodological strengths or clinical implications. Different teaching approaches may be useful to prevent sessions becoming monotonous and prescriptive for the members.

Formal teaching

As stated, the format of journal clubs is largely informal discussion. However, the inclusion of formal teaching sessions may be a helpful addition. This may be based specifically on the identified needs of the members. Similarly, if a series of papers on a specific research methodology is planned, then it may be advantageous to introduce the theme with a preliminary session on research methods and technical terminology. This may be particularly useful for areas such as diagnostic accuracy studies, where issues of sensitivity, specificity and likelihood ratios can be difficult to interpret. Furthermore, the provision of a short training programme on areas such as epidemiology and biostatistics can also act to maintain the attraction of a journal club (Alguire, 1998).

Formulating conclusions

Once the article or articles have been reviewed, it is important that the clinical implications and 'take home message' are clearly identified by the Chair person. This will ensure that the initial research question has been answered, or, if this was not possible, that an avenue for further study has been clearly defined. The Chair person should also prompt members to complete a checklist, or some form of documented reflection of the session, so that the meeting has been recorded in the member's portfolio as a CPD activity.

Devising further research questions

Before the meeting is closed, members should construct a research or CPD question for the following meeting. This may be based on an important clinical question or a need to devise a departmental policy. Alternatively, members may wish to study a particular research method or evaluate a topical paper or recently published guideline. If group members rotate the different journal club roles amongst themselves, this should be decided before the group disperses for the next meeting. Finally, if not pre-determined, the group should set a time and place for the next meeting.

Do journal clubs work?

The literature surrounding journal clubs is largely based on descriptive studies and process or review articles (Thompson, 2006). Studies assessing the efficacy of journal clubs have mostly been conducted with medical doctors (Alguire, 1998; Edwards *et al*, 2001; Parkes *et al*, 2010). Two randomised controlled trials have assessed the efficacy of journal clubs; both provide support for them. Firstly, Linzer *et al* (1988) reported that attendance at a journal club increased the critical appraisal skills and academic reading habits of its members, compared to people who only received a series of seminars on evidence-based medicine (Linzer *et al*, 1988). Secondly, Macraw *et al* (2004) similarly reported that those randomised to an internet-based journal club reported significantly greater critical appraisal skills on re-examination, compared to those who only received a series of academic papers. Further cohort studies have suggested that journal clubs, in addition to didactic research appraisal teaching, can significantly improve the critical appraisal skills and research methodological knowledge of junior doctors and medical students (Seeling, 1991; Carley *et al*, 1998; Kellum *et al*, 2000; Cramer and Mahoney, 2001; Edwards *et al*, 2001; Owen *et al*, 2001; Hartzell *et al*, 2009; Moharari *et al*, 2009). Similarly, in the nursing literature, Seff and Hales (1988), Fraser (1994), Sheehan (1994), Goodfellow (2004) and Thompson (2006) all reported positive findings with the introduction of journal clubs into nursing practice to foster critical appraisal skills.

No studies have specifically assessed the efficacy of journal clubs with post-registration physiotherapists or occupational therapists. Stern (2008) reported the experiences of 14 occupational therapy students who attended nine journal club sessions during their pre-registration training. She reported favourable comments from the students towards the journal club sessions. Students reported that the sessions enhanced their group leadership skills and their abilities to listen to fellow-group members' comments and made them feel like professionals (Stern, 2008). Students also reported that they felt journal clubs were a viable means of CPD for their future employment (Stern, 2008).

Whilst there is, therefore, limited evidence to support the use of journal clubs in the practice of post-registration allied health professions, Turner and Whitfield (1999) recommend that they should be mandatory for CPD within allied health profession departments, citing that they are widely acknowledged as an effective learning environment to promote evidence use, fostering critical evaluation of literature and analytical thinking (Stelmach, 1994; Sandifer *et al*, 1996).

Strengths and weaknesses of journal clubs

Lack of time and inadequate preparation are two key factors associated with the failure of journal clubs (Alam and Jawaid, 2009). Such clubs do require time out of clinical practice, particularly in their infancy, to ensure that members develop the necessary skills for article identification and critical appraisal. They also demand a level of commitment to ensure that the momentum of each meeting continues to the next session. As Taylor (2004) suggested, given the need to demonstrate clinical effectiveness, and the requirement for documented CPD for professional revalidation in UK physiotherapy and occupational therapy practice, managers and team leaders should encourage the establishment and maintenance of journal clubs for their employees. However, this is counterbalanced against caseload pressures, and should be considered a potential threat to the success of a journal club.

Journal clubs can also be perceived as boring and of limited practical use. In such cases, this may be attributed to the lack of a clearly defined purpose to the meetings or limited clinical applicability. If such a situation ensues or if the format of the group becomes stale, a re-assessment of the group's objectives, or re-assessment of the types of literature discussed, may be required to re-focus the meetings.

As a strength, journal clubs can inform the development of departmental policy, to permit a degree of shared decision-making about changes in practice. When used in this way, the club can be considered a beneficial tool to incorporate the different perceptions of members, particularly when assisting in the development of controversial or unpopular changes to practice (Bury and Jerosch-Herold, 1998).

Journal clubs can be co-ordinated and run anywhere. They need not be dependent on the proximity of a university, library or other educational establishment. With the advent of internet-based journal clubs, forums and social network sites (Macraw *et al*, 2004), journal clubs can be run by even the most geographically dispersed healthcare teams.

Finally, journal clubs can lead to further research or publication. Previous journal clubs have stimulated debate which has lead to the publication of letters pertaining to issues raised during meetings (Edwards *et al*, 2001). As well as developing the evidence-base on a topic, this is a further means of documenting CPD. Such publications can inspire members to continue their journal club learning. Furthermore, by examining an issue in detail, members are better able to determine the strengths and weaknesses of a topic's current evidence-base. This can then provide a springboard for interested members to undertake their own clinical research and audit. Through this, the journal club can provide a tangible change to clinical practice, whilst facilitating its members' life-long learning.

Conclusions

There is no single correct way to run a journal club. The expectations of a club's members will vary from practitioner to practitioner, dependent on workload pressures, the objectives of the club, and the member's own critical appraisal skills and CPD needs (Deenadeyalan *et al*, 2008). Members should therefore find what works best for them. Nevertheless, the recommendations made in this chapter on the roles and structure of a journal club should be considered to ensure that this resource for CPD activity works efficiently, and provides its members with a useful tool to develop their practice.

Key points

* A journal club is a group of practitioners who meet to present, appraise and discuss literature
* Journal clubs provide practitioners with an opportunity to discuss professional literature, to practise critical appraisal skills, and to demonstrate their CPD
* The selection of literature should be driven by patients' or learners' needs
* A checklist may be useful to ensure that each article is appropriately critiqued, and that the professional and personal implications are reflected upon
* Checklists can be used as a form of portfolio documentation to demonstrate CPD activity

References

AGREE (Appraisal of Guidelines Research and Evaluation) (2001) The AGREE appraisal instrument. Available at: http://www.agreecollaboration.org [Accessed 24 August 2010]

Alam SN, Jawaid M (2009) Journal clubs: An important teaching tool for postgraduates. *Journal of College of Physicians and Surgeons Pakistan* 19(2): 71–2

Alguire PC (1998) A review of journal clubs in postgraduate medical education. *Journal of General Internal Medicine* 13(5): 347–53

Allebeck P (2006) Necessary steps for a modern scientific journal. *European Journal of Public Health* 16(1): 1

Austin TM, Richter RR (2009) Using a partnership between academic faculty and a physical therapist liaison to develop a framework for an evidence-based journal club: A discussion. *Physiotherapy Research International* 14(4): 213–23

Bury T, Jerosch-Herold C (1998) Reading and critical appraisal of the literature. In: Bury T, Mead M eds. *Evidence-based healthcare: A practical guide for therapists.* Butterworth-Heinemann, Oxford: 136–61

Carley SD, Mackway-Jones K, Jones A, Morton RJ, Dollery W, Maurice S, Niklaus L, Donnan S (1998) Moving towards evidence based emergency medicine: Use of a structured critical appraisal journal club. *Journal of Accident and Emergency Medicine* 15(4): 220–6

Cramer JA, Mahoney MC (2001) Introducing evidence based medicine to the journal club, using a structured pre and post test: A cohort study. *BMC Medical Education* 1(1): 6

Cutcliffe J, Ward M (2007) *Critiquing nursing research.* Quay books, Gateshead, UK

Deenadayalan Y, Grimmer-Somers K, Prior M, Kumar S (2008) How to run an effective journal club: A systematic review. *Journal of Evaluation in Clinical Practice* 14(5): 898–911

Dubouloz C, Egan M, Vallerand J, von Zweck C (1999) Occupational therapists' perceptions of evidence-based practice. *American Journal of Occupational Therapy* 53(5): 445–53

Edwards R, White M, Gray J, Fischbacher C (2001) Use of a journal club and letter-writing exercise to teach critical appraisal to medical undergraduates. *Medical Education* 35(7): 691–4

Esdaile SA, Roth LM (2004) Creating scholarly practice: Integrating and applying scholarship to practice. In: Brown G, Esdaile SA, Ryan SE eds. *Becoming an advanced healthcare practitioner.* Butterworth Heinemann, London: 161–88

Fraser C (1994) Journal club for nursing students. *Nurse Education* **19**(3): 8–9

Goodfellow LM (2004) Can a journal club bridge the gap between research and practice? *Nurse Education* **29**(3): 107–10

Hartzell JD, Veerappan GR, Posley K, Shumway NM, Durning SJ (2009) Resident run journal club: A model based on the adult learning theory. *Medical Teaching* **31**(4): e156–e161

Health Professions Council (2009) *Continuing fitness to practise: Towards an evidence based approach to revalidation.* Health Professions Council, United Kingdom. Available at: http://www.hpc-uk.org/assets/documents/10002AAEContinuingfitnesst opractise-Towardsanevidence-basedapproachtorevalidation.pdf [Accessed 23 August 2010]

Kellum JA, Rieker JP, Poer M, Powner DJ (2000) Teaching critical appraisal during critical care fellowship training: A foundation for evidence-based critical care medicine. *Critical Care Medicine* **28**(8): 3067–70

Linzer M (1987) The journal club and medical education: Over one hundred years of unrecorded history. *Postgraduate Medical Journal* **63**(740): 475–8

Linzer M, Brown JT, Fraizer LM, DeLong ER, Siegel WC (1988) Impact of a medical journal club on house-staff reading habits, knowledge, and critical appraisal skills. A randomized controlled trial. *Journal of the American Medical Association* **260**(17): 2537–41

Macraw HM, Regehr G, McKenzie M, Henteleff H, Taylor M, Barkun J, Fitzgerald GW, Hill A, Richard C, Webber EM, McLeod RS (2004) Teaching practising surgeons critical appraisal skills with an Internet-based journal club: A randomized, controlled trial. *Surgery* **136**(3): 641–6

Maher CG, Sherrington C, Herbert RD, Moseley AM, Elkins M (2003) Reliability of the PEDro scale for rating quality of randomized controlled trials. *Physical Therapy* **83**(8): 713–21

Mensch J, Mitchell M (2003) Journal club as professional socialization. *Athlete Therapy Today* **8**(4): 68–70

Milbrandt EB, Vincent J-L (2004) Evidence-based medicine journal club. *Critical Care* **8**(6): 401–2

Moharari RS. Rahimi E, Najafi A, Khashayar P, Khajavi MR, Meysamie AP (2009) Teaching critical appraisal and statistics in anaesthesia journal club. *Quarterly Journal of Medicine* **102**(2): 139–41

Morton SA (1996) Setting up a journal club. *Health Visitor* **69**(11): 465–6

Owen S, Wheway J, Anderson M (2001) The use of a journal club and clinical seminars on a 4-year undergraduate, pre-registration mental-health nursing degree. *Nurse Education Today* **21**(4): 297–303

Paget S (1901) *Memoirs and letters of Sir James Paget.* Longmans, Green and Co, London

Parkes J, Hyde C, Deeks J, Milne R (2010) *Teaching critical appraisal skills in health care settings.* Cochrane Library, Issue I

Public Health Resource Unit (PHRU) (2007) *The Critical Appraisal Skills Programme appraisal tools.* Available at: http://www.phru.nhs.uk/pages/phd/resources.htm [Accessed 24 August 2010]

Sandifer QD, Lo S, Crompton PG (1996) Evaluation of a journal club as a forum to practice critical appraisal skills. *Journal of the Royal College of Physicians of London* **30**(6): 520–2

Seeling CB (1991) Affecting residents' literature reading attitudes, behaviors, and knowledge through a journal club intervention. *Journal of General Internal Medicine* **6**(4): 330–4

Seff SE, Hales S (1988) Journal club: A teaching strategy in RN education. *Journal of Nurse Education* **27**(3): 135–6

Sheehan J (1994) A journal club as a teaching and learning strategy. *Journal of Advanced Nursing* **19**(3): 572–8

Sherratt C (2005) The journal club: A method for occupational therapists to bridge the theory-practice gap. *British Journal of Occupational Therapy* **68**(7): 301–6

Stelmach EI (1994) A staff journal club as a method of continuing education. *AORN Journal of Continuing Education* **59**(5): 1061–3

Stern P (2008) Using journal clubs to promote skills for evidence-based practice. *Occupational Therapy Health Care* **22**(4): 36–53

Straus SE, Richardson WS, Glasziou P, Haynes RB (2005) *Evidence-based medicine. How to practice and teach EBM.* 3rd edn. Elsevier Churchill Livingstone, London

Taylor MC (2000) *Evidence-based practice for occupational therapists.* Blackwell Sciences, Oxford

Taylor MC (2004) Evidence-based practice: Informing practice and critically evaluating related research. In: Brown G, Esdaile SA, Ryan SE eds. *Becoming an advanced healthcare practitioner.* Butterworth Heinemann, London: 90–117

Thompson CJ (2006) Fostering skills for evidence-based practice. The student journal club. *Nurse Education in Practice* **6**(2): 69–77

Turner PA, Mjolne I (2001) Journal provision and prevalence of journal club within physiotherapy departments: A survey of facilities in England and Australia. *Physiotherapy Research International* **6**(3): 157–69

Turner PA, Whitfield TWA (1999) Physiotherapists' reasons for selection of treatment techniques: A cross-national survey. *Physiotherapy Theory and Practice* **15**(4): 235–46

Chapter 10

Practice education and CPD

Introduction
Catherine Wells

Amidst the shifting sands of health and social care policies and practice it would seem that there are two significant topics which underpin healthcare delivery – quality and productivity (Department of Health, 2011). Regardless of how service details are configured, the workforce, both those currently practising and those of the future, need to underpin their activity with these concepts, striving towards best practice.

Quality practice is aspired to through the use of evidence, efficiency, professional development and accountability at the front line of delivery. Productivity is addressed through effectiveness, getting it right first time and facilitating an environment where improvement can flourish. When considering the responsibilities of developing the future workforce, existing practitioners need to consider how they can best meet these remits through the delivery of practice education, engendering good practice in their approach to educating students, as well as reflecting this quality standard within their own working practices. The task presents a key opportunity to integrate development, thus serving two distinct but inter-related purposes – education of the self and education of the student.

The perspective of meeting more than one objective from an activity suits the quality agenda. In an era where evidence of CPD is a key component of continuing to practice (Health Professions Council 2006), the process of educating students on practice demonstrates not only the development of the practice educator, but also of the student. Frequently these are seen as discrete activities, yet a little thought and exploration enables the single task to meet both targets – the whole process of educating students leads the educators to reflect on their own practice, and to evaluate their effectiveness (Mann *et al* 2009). Evidence from the task can be used to support registration from a statutory body, and to meet the requirement for lifelong learning (Department of Health 2001, College of Occupational Therapists, 2002), it also potentially addresses a practitioner's grade and job description (Department of Health, 2004).

This chapter explores the context for practice education, and considers the roles and responsibilities of the practice educator and, from this, suggests evidence of CPD for the personnel involved. Through following the processes of practice education it aims to make explicit links between activities and CPD, providing a format which not only assures good practice but also suggests a model of how to gather pertinent evidence. The chapter does not seek to provide a recipe, however. Whilst there are key activities undertaken, it is the way the evidence is interpreted and worked upon which provides the individual's material for demonstrating his or her own professional development through using the process of student education in a structured manner.

Terminology

The shift in terminology from fieldwork practice, to fieldwork education and subsequently practice education reflects a mind shift in terms of the process and purpose of this component of the student's training. The emphasis on education moves the activity from one which was focused on technique, to one where knowledge, skills and attitudes are developed as part of becoming a competent practitioner, equipped for a challenging and varied workplace environment. Education is paralleled in the development of the educator, reflecting the ethos of lifelong learning, which in itself provides evidence of change. The change of language links to the changing context for student experience, where traditional placements offer new opportunity and non-traditional placements facilitate development in areas where the student's own profession may not be part of the service. The interpretation of the learning experience is a key role for the student's educator, providing essential evidence of development.

This chapter suggests that there are four significant areas of engagement for practice educators that are able to evidence CPD, namely their preparatory training, preparation for the student, the process of using the self in educating the student and evaluation of the activities as evidence of change. These underpin the purpose of a placement which is to acquire professional knowledge, skills and attitudes, to integrate theory and practice and to develop professional identity (Waters, 2001). Throughout the process, some CPD activity can be recorded as knowledge gained externally, whilst much is acquired through demonstrating everyday practice. The categories will be explored giving a summary of suggested CPD evidence, emphasising that this is a parallel process of development for both parties, i.e. the student and the practice educator.

Training

The importance of the task is reflected in a change of emphasis within practice education courses, with these resulting in professional body accreditation, academic credit or compliance with individual job descriptions. Whilst each course is individually developed the following learning outcomes offer guiding principles for constructing the training and evaluating the performance of delegates. These focus on:

- The role and attributes of the effective practice educator
- The application of learning theories that are appropriate for adult and professional learners
- Planning, implementing and facilitating learning in the practice setting
- Application of sound principles and judgement in the assessment of the student's performance
- Evaluation of the learning experience
- Reflection of the experience and the formulation of action plans for future practice. (Accreditation of Practice Placement Educators Scheme, College of Occupational Therapists, 2005; Accreditation of Clinical Educators Scheme, Chartered Society of Physiotherapy, 2004.)

Completing the training days and demonstrating evidence of the above learning outcomes allows some professions to apply for professional body accreditation, thus acquiring recognition of the learning experience. Where this formal recognition is not available, practice educators are able to use the training opportunity to provide evidence of the learning that has taken place, documenting it in their portfolio. The temptation from any such learning opportunity may be to submit a certificate of attendance. However, individuals should ask themselves if this actually provides evidence of development, or merely evidence of attendance.

Lifelong learning implies continuing activity, and an understanding that practice educators are cognizant of their developmental needs, thus being proactive in accessing further opportunity. These might be workshops on key topics, for example, challenging students, community working, clinical reasoning or making judgements on assessment. These have the potential for developing learning which is only valuable if it can be applied to individual practice, thus effecting change.

Table 10.1. Practice educator development	
Training activity	**Potential CPD evidence**
Practice educator course	Assessment of learning outcomes Accreditation, academic credit, complying with the job description Entry to practice educator register
Post-course training	Identifying training needs, taking responsibility for addressing these Training events – evidencing ways in which individual practice has developed

Preparation for the student

Learning environments have developed in response to health and social care provision, offering an opportunity for practitioners to negotiate, plan and implement student experience in both traditional and non-traditional settings. Preparing for the student is a critical activity which ensures that the placement offers a suitable learning experience, one which makes use of the personnel and facilities available, and which addresses the student's objectives as well as those of the service. A primary CPD activity that educators undertake relates to showcasing their particular service, marketing this in a way which engages students and provides them with essential information in preparation for their experience. The use of outdated, limited information which fails to fully inform the student misses a critical opportunity and reflects negatively upon the organisation.

It is worth considering the quality of this first communication with the student and assessing the areas it addresses. Is the organisation explained sufficiently to enable the student to have a grasp of its purpose? Is the team reflected as a group of experts with specific skills? Are the learning opportunities current? Have practicalities been addressed so the student can actually find the department and the accommodation? What is the student to access prior to the placement, and is this a reasonable expectation? A lengthy booklist cannot not be read, however an article, a Government paper or a chapter suggests a much more realistic approach to preparation, as these are manageable for the student. Taking time to review this process, and updating it as required provides an appropriate and timely piece of portfolio evidence.

Within preparation it is useful to consider the wider environment within which students will undertake their placements, and the learning opportunities which these offer. Services rarely function in isolation, therefore scoping links across teams, agencies, professions and sectors results in students accessing learning opportunities which can be evidenced as an educational rather than simply a practice experience. Students will recount a visit or time with a professional as a positive experience, but may need prompting to understand why that was a pertinent part of their learning on that particular placement. Educators have the opportunity to consider the value of an opportunity offered to the student, and what evidence of learning they are expecting from that engagement, therefore evaluating its purpose and developing their knowledge.

Planning extends to considering the formal learning as well as the experiential learning for the student. Many departments have a menu of tutorials, involving

Table 10.2. Preparation for the student	
Planning activity	**Potential CPD evidence**
Pre-placement information for the student	Showcase the service Information about the team Current learning opportunities in the wider environment Formal learning opportunities Up-to-date practical information Realistic preparatory reading
Planning the programme	Evaluating learning opportunities and developing a method of valuing their involvement in student education Formalising inter-professional links to provide formal education opportunities across groups of students Ensuring all contacts are up to date and that their role within the student's programme is purposeful

colleagues delivering sessions to students which tend to be uni-professional and to a sole student. Some preparatory planning should identify which other student learners could benefit from this opportunity, so that shared professional activity is not limited to hands-on patient contact, but also encompasses the theory which underpins practice. This sharing may be more practical in some areas than others, but it is worthy of the question as to why students and practitioners from different disciplines work together on wards, yet rely on their own professions for clinical tutorials. If services are to embrace the directive of working more productively with fewer resources, then it makes sense to develop an inter-professional menu of current learning topics which can be delivered by a range of practitioners and attended by groups of learners.

Time spent at the planning stage of a placement may initially be seen as a time-consuming activity, one which further complicates the responsibility of taking students and which requires some dedicated energy. However, it is an activity which then frees the educator during the actual placement and results in the students accessing a quality learning experience.

The process of practice education

The process of practice education is reliant upon quality preparation, and is the 'hands on' learning which occurs when the student undertakes the placement. This will be guided by the desired outcomes, formally from the academic institution and personally from the student who should be aware of his or her individual learning goals. The role of the educator is to facilitate the learning experience to encompass both sets of objectives, and to assess the student's performance at the stage of training reached. This is a critical role which is demonstrated through the following qualities:

- Being an effective communicator (Hummell, 1997; Milner and Bossers, 2004)
- Demonstrating artistry and technical excellence in practice (Strohschein *et al*, 2002; McAllister and Lincoln, 2004)
- Being a facilitator of development (Kirke *et al*, 2007; Lawson and Klaentschi, 2006)
- Being a role model (Mulholland *et al*, 2006; Overton *et al*, 2009)
- Being committed to professional development (Blanchard and Aziz, 2002; Higgs and McAllister, 2005).

These qualities can be seen within the whole process of practice education, and, as they provide evidence of the continuing ability of the educator, are worthy of exploration to enable them to contribute potential evidence of development.

Effective communication

The process of facilitating practice education and the development of the student is a very personal commitment, one which relies on good communication between those involved. The communication network for the practice educator is extensive, demonstrated through the wider clinical and educational environment, the workplace environment and centrally with the student. The complexity of this task is perhaps taken for granted, and, because it forms part of the daily requirements of the practitioner, it is assumed that it meets the right standards. It is easy, within a busy work schedule, to follow existing patterns of communication for practice education which may be outdated or lack currency. The communication qualities which students consider as important in their practice educator include interpersonal communication which is flexible, supportive, respectful, and where their contributions are listened to (Hummell, 1997). Additionally, they seek constructive criticism and that the expectations of them are clarified to prevent misunderstandings (Kirke *et al,* 2007), thus encouraging deep learning as opposed to superficial instruction. The skill of educators lies in adapting their verbal and non-verbal communication skills to the task – through providing information, supporting students, judging their performance and providing feedback to justify the assessment, all of which are sources of development.

Artistry and technical competence in practice

This liberating concept was considered almost a decade ago by Strohschein *et al* (2002) to be one of the goals of practice education for a healthcare professional. For students to develop this balance between artistry and technical skill they require teachers who can demonstrate this within their own practice. It is tempting for the educator to focus on the quest for technical competence, creating a programme of learning where the student will be able to demonstrate competent technical skills. This will be a safe and secure learning experience, but it may lack the flexibility and fluidity of facilitating deeper learning beyond the expected practice. Professional artistry relates to the ways in which therapists use the self and their professional knowledge to weave together the components of a therapeutic intervention, an active role which uses observation, communication, participation, with implicit evidence provided through theoretical foundations, clinical reasoning and reflective practice (Atkinson and Wells, 2000). This artistry has to be contained within a secure boundary, but does provide an opportunity to question and develop practice in a critical manner. The toolbox of skills that accompanies the educator needs to demonstrate a balance of these qualities, recognising that whilst practice may be developed using technical competence, there is a place for artistry within the process. Evidence is acquired through reflecting on both components, thus thinking about how an educator teaches practice, what contributes to the learning process and whether this results in deep or superficial learning.

Facilitating student development

The role of the practice educator is to develop students' competence to enable them to reach the practice standards of proficiency expected of a registered professional (Health Professions Council, 2006). The process involves developing clinical reasoning skills through the integration of theory and practice, plus the process of using practice to inform theory. To facilitate development, the practice educator undertakes three supervisory roles; a managerial role, a supportive role and an educative role (Kilminster and Jolly, 2000) which results in a judgement about the level of the student's performance.

The managerial role

The practice educator undertakes the responsibility of planning the student's learning, implementing and assessing learning using appropriate feedback and evaluation, and using learner feedback to enhance quality practice (Morris and Moore, 2006). These are student-focused activities around competence which have to be managed within the context of the organisation. Each placement experience will be built around the learning outcomes for that placement, plus the student's individual learning goals, and it is the management of these within the day-to-day activity and ethos of the placement provider that will be addressed through the supervision process. Students may, for example, have an unrealistic learning objective or consider that they can have access to opportunities which are not feasible but which need to be discussed to provide the reasoning which precludes engaging in these activities. The presence of students needs to be managed in relation to their impact on the existing team or the service, and formal supervision sessions provide an appropriate place to discuss some of the implications of behaviour. As part of the student's programme the practice educator manages these supervision sessions, establishing them as a regular part of the weekly activity and preserving this time for its agreed purpose. This involves the provision of a suitable private space as well as a time commitment to prepare for, undertake and reflect on the process of developing learning.

The practice educator will also have a responsibility in relation to management of the paperwork which accompanies the placement. This constitutes vital evidence of the student's performance, but also offers an opportunity for CPD evidence, for example where the educator reflects upon, and subsequently changes their day-to-day practice in managing the student's learning.

The supportive role

Support during practice education broadly falls into two components – that which is focused on individual students, recognising their personal investment in the process, and that which enhances clinical competence, recognising that this is a purposeful learning environment with set objectives.

Students are under a variety of pressures as they undertake a new practice experience. They are often away from their normal support network, in strange accommodation, a new location, and may be the only student from their higher education institution (HEI). Whilst it is reasonable to argue that these are mature adults undertaking further education, there needs to be some recognition from the skilled educator that these challenges may impact on and can compromise practice learning. This does not mean taking responsibility for the student away from the clinical area, but it does mean taking an active role in pre-empting some of the potential difficulties. It is useful, for example, for students to have information about leisure activities, shopping resources, medical facilities, etc. An advantage of a more regional approach to placements and the emphasis on inter-professional education can result in students from the same HEI on different programmes coming together at a placement site. This can partly be facilitated within the HEI, but it can also be enhanced through a greater recognition of the multiple student presence within a provider organisation.

The pressure of being judged may prevent students from honestly discussing their personal issues, as they perceive these as being weaknesses which potentially reflect negatively on their performance. Interpersonal skills are a key quality for the practice educator to employ, thus supporting the student in disclosing personal issues which may be compromising their learning. For this to be a safe activity there need to be some boundaries and ground rules on both sides with a genuine commitment to engaging in the process, recognising that the purpose is support through supervision rather than therapy (Hawkins and Shohet, 2007). Boundaries create a facilitating environment (Daniel and Blair, 2002), therefore the educator needs to establish the process of the activity in terms of time, commitment and expectation thus avoiding misunderstandings which compromise the purpose of facilitating learning. Good supervision, as identified by Spence *et al* (2001), creates a relationship which is 'nurturing, supportive, interactive, welcoming and safe enough for open disclosure from both parties'. It encourages an active, as opposed to a passive role thus enabling students to own and address their problems rather than negating responsibility. Respect underpins the relationship; respect both for students disclosing to their educators, and from educators in supporting rather than solving the issues as they arise. Reflection on the ways in which students receive support, the quality of support given and whether this addresses the issue provides a critique of the experience, demonstrating development both for students and their educators.

The educative role

The educative role encompasses not only the day-to-day learning which occurs throughout the placement, but also the formal points where the student's performance is assessed. Both of these key responsibilities are described by Fieldhouse and Fedden (2009: 302) as 'unlocking the learning potential of the setting'. To facilitate learning it is important that educators are self-aware, and so have identified their own learning style, understanding the ways in which they respond to a learning situation. As they undertake their role they will encounter students who bring with them the whole range of learning styles, from the activist, who is keen to get on with the job, to the theorist, who examines the reasoning behind the proposed action, to the reflector, who thinks about how things should be achieved, to the pragmatist, who tends towards a realistic approach for getting the actions under way (Honey and Mumford, 1992). The student's approach may be different from that of the educator. Using the induction process both to help students identify their own styles of learning, and as an opportunity to discuss educators' preferred style will generate understanding of the differences, and present an opportunity for planning for these differences, rather than letting them compromise development for either party.

Supervision aims to enhance students' knowledge of the clinical presentations they are involved with. Within this protected, student-focused time this knowledge will be developed through discussion of the therapeutic process to increase technical proficiency, but it will also encompass problem solving skills, creativity, self-awareness and confidence towards undertaking a clinical activity (Spence *et al*, 2001). The process encourages reflection of the situations which arise during the practice placement, and are therefore distanced from the day-to-day, case-by-case, discussion which occurs as part of the daily learning. Within personal supervision, practice educators may not have all the answers to the issues which arise, but they provide the venue for discussion based on their own advanced clinical skills and professional knowledge.

Education within supervision needs to be purposeful and will involve some learning tasks. The aim is to assist students in achieving not only their individual learning goals, but also those set by the HEI for the specific placement. Skilled educators value evidence of students' learning, making time to read reflections and constructively comment on their development. Through this process a deeper level of learning is achieved, shifting the superficial discussion into an in-depth exploration to support learning. If supervision is seen as a joint learning process then students have to take responsibility for identifying their needs and should develop the skills of negotiation, but this is not easy in the early stages of developing professional confidence. Trust between the practice educator and the student within the supervisory relationship is essential to the process as the acquisition of new learning may, at times, raise anxiety (Daniel and Blair, 2002).

Assessment of performance is the judgemental component of facilitating the student's education. Whilst educators are charged with awarding a summative mark informed by the student's performance it is the comments which underpin and justify this mark which form important learning evidence for both student and educator. These validate the decision making process, and are a source for monitoring development of both parties, as evidence can be documented through observation, discussion, guided practice, tutorials, and the use of CPD tools such as reflective accounts, SWOT-B analysis and critical incident reporting.

129

Professional role model

Being a professional role model is an essential component of practice education. Students are exposed to a range of role models through working with different practice educators as they experience placement learning. This exposure is an essential part of the process and purpose of practice education (Overton *et al*, 2009) and it cannot be replicated within any other environment. The practice educator is the key role model for the student, and this somewhat nebulous persona is identified as a professional who is competent to practice with enthusiasm for the profession (Kirke *et al*, 2007), who has a sense of self and a sense of agency (Higgs and McAllister, 2005) and who demonstrates appropriate positive personal qualities (Milner and Bossers, 2004; Mullholland *et al*, 2006)

Effective practice educators should have reached a stage of confidence in their own knowledge base and practice to be able to demonstrate, question and provide evidence for their professional intervention when working with their students. The professional knowledge of the eductor will interpret the learning opportunities of the placement, informed by the client group, the interventions used, and the resources available. It will include teaching sessions, reflection and supervision, all of which should have the goal of developing and enhancing both the student's and the educator's knowledge, recognising that this is a process of continuous development which is constantly updated and documented.

The sense of self and sense of agency are personal attributes which provide an additional dimension to the professional knowledge base which practice educators demonstrate. The sense of self is evident in the ways in which practice educators perceive their role, which encompasses their values and identity. Imparting these qualities may be less intentional, but they are demonstrated through the context of practice where values, attitudes and the ability to practice professionally are significant attributes. This sense of self is evident within relationships with others, so the commitment to students on a personal as well as an educative level is valued, although the investment has to be balanced with the competing demands of relationships with colleagues and clients.

A sense of agency develops from the sense of self to consider professional confidence and competence within the context of the workplace, and refers to how professionals see themselves and the types of relationships they value (Higgs and McAllister, 2005). The sense of agency is evident within the management of the multiple tasks of facilitating student education, providing a learning environment, managing the self and others within the process, being aware of clinical responsibilities, and recognising negative emotions and attitudes. The complexity of developing an awareness not only of the self, but of the impact of the self demonstrates a level of expertise which students value as they relate this to genuineness, and to the positive interpersonal qualities of communication, non-verbal behaviours, honesty and openness.

Commitment to CPD

Commitment is the core quality which encapsulates the whole process of practice education and draws the threads of the learning experience together to provide a valuable experience for both student and educator. The previous internal qualities considered – communication, demonstrating artistry and excellence in practice, facilitating student development, being a role model and demonstrating positive interpersonal skills – all require a commitment to developing the performance of practice educators in parallel to developing the student. These two roles are synonymous; one should not and cannot occur without the other if we are to demonstrate the value of this role and the importance of truly educating students as opposed to just letting them practise. Equally, if practice educators are going to value the learning within the student, so should they value the learning which occurs within themselves as this task is undertaken. It gives evidence of a commitment to exploring best practice and to developing the confidence both professionally and personally to instigate change.

CPD is an integral part of statutory and professional agendas as a mechanism for assuring quality practice. Practice educators with a commitment to CPD welcome the opportunity to educate students, they are receptive to exploring and explaining practice, recognising and sharing the strengths and weaknesses of the system and being open-minded in recognising that practice may benefit from change and review. These educators treat all students as individuals, they generate programmes of learning in response to their students' needs and the opportunities of the service, they are interested in student development through engaging in learning events, and they facilitate feedback through encouraging students to reflect on the educator's performance, as well as their own. These practice educators demonstrate a passion for the task which is infectious and explicit, but they also use the experience for their own agenda, through reflection on the experience and the gathering of selective evidence of their development.

Table 10.3. Facilitating the learning experience	
Qualities of the practice educator	**Potential CPD evidence**
To be an effective communicator	Up-to-date information Evidence from effective listening Records of constructive, balanced feedback on performance
To demonstrate artistry and technical excellence in practice	Examples of clinical reasoning Re-thinking and questioning practice Evaluation of learning outcomes
To be a facilitator of development	Exploring learning styles Management of the placement learning experience Supporting mechanisms, supervision documentation, assessment justification
To be a role model	Evidence of the use of self Confidence and competence in practice Professional knowledge, skills, attitudes and judgements Commitment to the task Honest reflection
To be committed to professional development	A realistic approach to CPD activities through use of time and expertise Interpretation of opportunity for multiple evidence Reflection on task Recognition that CPD is an intrinsic element of workforce development to meet the professional and statutory quality standards

In summary, this chapter offers a tangible opportunity for practice educators to utilise the experience of educating students for their own development. Educating the future workforce remains a critical professional responsibility, and is one which is beset with issues around capacity. If the process can be explicitly recognised as achieving education for both the student and the practice educator, then this may raise the value and profile of the task, so that the delivery of practice education becomes a regular developmental activity rather than an occasional task. In this way students and their educators will benefit from the investment, and both will have a ready source of meaningful evidence of their own development throughout the experience.

Key points

- Practice education provides valuable evidence of development for both the student and the practice educator
- Practice education integrates theory into practice, and practice informs theory
- Practice education is an important learning experience for both the practice educator and the student
- Skilled practice education facilitates a quality learning experience

References

Atkinson K, Wells C (2000) *Creative therapies: a psychodynamic approach within occupational therapy.* Stanley Thornes, Cheltenham

Blanchard V, Aziz-Anjam S (2002) Fieldwork education is like a marmalade sandwich *Occupational Therapy News* **10**(1): 12

Chartered Society of Physiotherapy (2004) Accreditation of Clinical Educators Scheme (ACE). CSP, London

College of Occupational Therapists (2002) Position statement on lifelong learning. *British Journal of Occupational Therapy* **65**(5): 198–200

College of Occupational Therapists (2005) *Accreditation of Practice Placement Educators' Scheme (APPLE).* British Association of Occupational Therapists, London

Daniel M, Blair S (2002) A psychodynamic approach to clinical supervision. *British Journal of Therapy and Rehabilitation* **9**(6): 237–40

Department of Health (2001) *Working together – Learning together: A framework for Lifelong Learning for the NHS*. DoH, London

Department of Health (2004) *Agenda for change*. DOH, Leeds

Department of Health (2010) *The NHS quality, innovation, productivity and prevention: An introduction for clinicians*. DoH, London

Department of Health (2011) *Liberating the NHS: Developing the future health care workforce*. DoH, Leeds

Fieldhouse J, Fedden T (2009) Exploring the learning process on a role emergent practice placement: A qualitative study. *British Journal of Occupational Therapy* **72**(7): 302–7

Hawkins P, Shohet R (2007) *Supervision in the helping professions*. Open University Press, Berkshire

Health Professions Council (2005) *Standards of proficiency*. HPC, London

Health Professions Council (2006) *Standards for continuing professional development*. HPC, London

Higgs J, McAllister L (2005) The lived experience of clinical educators with implications for their preparation, support and professional development. *Learning in Health and Social Care* **4**(3): 156–71

Honey P, Mumford A (1992) *The manual of learning styles*. Peter Honey, Maidenhead

Hummell J (1997) Effective fieldwork supervision: OT student perspectives. *Australian Occupational Therapy Journal* **44**(4): 147–57

Kilminster S, Jolly B (2000) Effective supervision in clinical practice settings: A literature review. *Medical Education* **34**(10): 827–40

Kirke P Layton N, Sim J (2007) Informing fieldwork design, key elements to quality in fieldwork education for undergraduate occupational therapy students. *Australian Journal of Occupational Therapy* **54**(Issue Suppl s1): 13–22

Lawson K, Klaentschi C (2006) How to provide the best placement. *Therapy Weekly* **33**(15): 7–9

Mann K, Gordon J, Macleod A (2009) Reflection and reflective practice in health professions education: A systematic review. *Advances in Health Science Education* **14**(4): 595–621

McAllister L, Lincoln M (2004) *Clinical education in speech-language pathology*. Whurr, London

Milner T, Bossers A (2004) Evaluation of the mentor–mentee relationship in an occupational therapy mentorship programme. *Occupational Therapy International* **11**(2):

96–111

Morris J, Moore A (2006) Management of student placements. In Jones R, Jenkins F, eds. *Developing the allied health professional.* Radcliffe Publishing, Oxford

Mulholland S, Derdall M, Roy B (2006) The students' perspective on what makes an exceptional practice placement educator. *British Journal of Occupational Therapy* **69**(12): 567–71

Overton A, Clark M, Thomas Y (2009) A review of non-traditional OT practice placement education: A focus on role emergent and project placements. *British Journal of Occupational Therapy* **72**(7): 294–301

Spence S, Wilson J, Kavanagh D, Strong J, Worrall L (2001) Clinical supervision in four mental health professions: A review of the evidence. *Behaviour Change* **18**(3): 135–55

Strohschein J, Hagler P, May L (2002) Assessing the need for change in clinical education practices. *Physical Therapy* **82**(2): 160–72

Waters B (2001) Radical action for radical plans. *British Journal of Occupational Therapy* **64**(2): 577–8

Chapter 11

Spiritual and transpersonal developments within occupational therapy education

Introduction

Mick Collins

Spirituality within healthcare practice is recognised as making an important contribution to patients' experiences of well-being (Daaleman *et al*, 2001). The links between spirituality and health have been acknowledged by the World Health Organization (Culliford, 2002), as well as being recognised within the UK National Health Service (NHS) in the Department of Health publication *Standards for better health* (Department of Health, 2004). These developments have identified that the connection between spirituality and health is a concern for all health professions (Collins, 2006). However, it is instructive to note that Koenig's (2004) investigations into the typical barriers that prevent health professionals engaging with spirituality in practice include lack of time, disinterest, or discomfort with the subject. This highlights that there is much work to be done before health professionals are confident in integrating spirituality more fully into practice, alongside the bio-psycho-social determinants of health (Whipp, 1998). Therefore, understanding the educational and training needs of health professionals to facilitate the integration of spirituality within practice is highly pertinent (Koenig, 2004).

Since the mid-1990s there has been international interest in developing spirituality within the profession of occupational therapy (OT), linking theory to practice (Egan and De Laat, 1994; Christiansen, 1997; Collins, 1998; Unruh *et al*, 2002). Occupational therapists have contributed to quality research, which has focused on the benefits of considering spirituality in patient care (do Rozario, 1997; McColl *et al*, 2000; Schulz, 2005). However, there is still much uncertainty and ambivalence amongst OTs about integrating spirituality into practice, whilst also acknowledging its relevance (Wilson, 2010). This highlights an important issue in terms of OT education and training in the UK, which is based on the long-standing recognition that spirituality needs to be more fully developed in terms of education to prepare students for professional practice to bridge what Belcham (2004) has described as the theory–practice gap. My particular interest in writing this chapter has evolved from a long-standing interest in the subject, where I integrated spirituality into my therapeutic practice (Collins, 1998). Now, as an educator, I am exploring how spirituality can be delivered within an OT curriculum. In this chapter I discuss the development of a six week module that considered theoretical and practical developments linked to spirituality within the education of third year OT students at the University of East Anglia. The students' reflections on the six week module were an important part of teaching evaluation, and the feedback has been organised into three themes: (1) reflections with others, (2) reflections on self, and (3) reflections on practice.

Spirituality, education, and reflection: where did I start?

The development of the module was focused on the need to prepare students to reflect on spirituality in OT practice, which was centred on their CPD needs. Existing research into the educational needs of OT students found that they did not feel prepared to address spirituality within practice placements, suggesting that spirituality needs to be further developed within OT education (Csontó, 2009). There are very few examples in the published literature that have outlined relevant course content for teaching spirituality to OT students. I was inspired by two key publications, both from Canada, which addressed issues of learning and reflection in relation to spirituality and occupational therapy. The first is a learner-centred workbook, *Spirituality in enabling occupation* (Townsend *et al*, 1999), which provides some useful reflective exercises on the subject of spirituality, and highlights the importance of self-reflection and development. The second publication by Kirsch *et al* (2001) is a qualitative research article, which has illustrated examples of how spirituality is considered in OT education in Canada; revealing how the participants were facilitated to gain a 'deeper understanding of their own spirituality'. These publications gave a clear indication that reflection should play an important role in the educational process within the module that I was developing. Moreover, a study carried out by Barry and Gibbens (2011) has revealed how combined study and reflection contributed to students' personal and professional development.

The challenge of using reflection to address the subject of spirituality within the education of health professionals is put into a dynamic context by Wright (1998) and Pain (2005), who have both stated that professionals can only work safely with the spiritual needs of clients if they have reflected on the question of spirituality within their own lives. These observations have highlighted the importance of OTs being active and accountable for their professional development in order to be competent to manage issues to do with spirituality in practice (Kang, 2003). The importance of using reflection to develop spirituality within the curriculum prompted me to consider ways in which the students could be involved in taking responsibility for their personal and professional development in relation to their thoughts, reactions, and behaviours (Cottrell, 2003).

It has been recognised that being a therapist creates opportunities for continuing emotional, intellectual and spiritual growth (Kottler, 1986); however, such aspirations are tempered by the realisation that the process of transforming practice can only occur if the therapist is willing to engage in a reflective journey (Wright, 1998). Furthermore, Wright (1998) has asserted that the process of reflection itself has the potential to initiate a spiritual journey through questioning and understanding who we are as practitioners and human beings, which can have an impact on identity and development (Collins, 2001). The view that active reflection is important when considering spirituality within professional development concurs with the observation made by Kolb (1984) who identified that learning requires more than experience alone, which situates reflection as 'an essential part of professional practice' (Bulpitt and Martin, 2005).

The development of the course content required careful consideration and selection of the core themes that were to be addressed, which underscored the need to make clear links between theory and practice (Belcham, 2004). The educational foundations for the module were based on the following considerations:

* Use of a range of teaching and learning styles to accommodate students' diverse learning needs (Jarvis, 2005), and to make the teaching material interesting and dynamic
* The adoption of a creative approach and attitude to the learning experience (Cowley, 2005), including the sharing of thoughts, experiences and ideas with others, which are recognised as stimulating the process of self-reflection (Boden, 1990).
* Assurance that the teaching material is delivered authentically by the educator (Hollis, 2000; Ramsden, 2003), which included interacting with the students in ways that encouraged their authentic engagement with the material being studied (Cranton and Carusetta, 2004).

- Encouragement of reflection commensurate with professional practice (Schön, 1987) including the use of CPD activity and tools (Department of Health, 2000) to support the students' process of learning and reflection.
- Provision of a safe environment that encourages students to examine and explore their experiences (Boyd and Fales, 1983), which in turn could provide opportunities for authentic reflection related to their chosen vocation (Regan, 2008).

Structuring the process of learning and reflection

The structure of the six week module was designed to enable students to engage with theoretical knowledge and their own experiences, which included reflections on the boundaries between personal and professional spheres of self. I was aware that my role as an educator needed to convey clear intentions about the design of the course, which was explicitly focused on the students having opportunities to encounter their own spiritual beliefs and values, or lack of them. I recognised that I had to take account of the fact that such a personal level of reflective engagement had the potential to inform a deep and dynamic approach within the students' learning experiences, as opposed to a surface engagement with knowledge (Cannon and Newble, 2000). The six week module was designed to stimulate and engage students, with the aim of fostering a 'genuine interest in knowledge' (Jarvis, 2005). However, when opportunities for personal reflection are factored into learning, such activities need to be engaged responsibly and ethically as noted by Hobbs (2007), who cautioned against any type of coercion in the reflective process. Thus, opportunities for self-examination need to be treated with care and respect, based on the understanding that there is always the possibility of encountering an 'affective dimension' when entering into a process of deep reflection (Brew, 2006).

I anticipated that enabling reflection in the context of a dynamic learning environment could highlight tensions in the course design; between the emotional well-being of the students, and the value of positive risk taking. This potential dichotomy was exacerbated by the possibility that dynamic reflections on the subject of spirituality could elicit tensions between the personal and professional boundaries of the self. The learning approach that I used in the design of the modules placed most of the emphasis on the students' gauging the amount of self-examination/revelation in terms of their personal learning experiences. The structure of the course took account of the potential for awkward responses and reactions to self-disclosure (Delega *et al*, 1993), which was tempered by the intention to create an educational milieu that encouraged productive sharing between students based on mutual respect for diverse opinions. Furthermore, Delega *et al* (1993) have noted that self-disclosure within productive relationships can have a transformative effect. Whilst I was aware that any level of meaningful engagement in the learning process could potentially be transformative (Kolb, 1984; Moon, 2000), I also acknowledged that once the students' educational and emotional needs had been considered, it is the students themselves who decide the depth and scope of their involvement and the level of their personal contributions to sessions. In such instances, learning is only transformative 'if the learner chooses to engage in such activities' (Ponton *et al*, 2005).

Based on the discussion outlined above, I designed the content for the six week module on the following core themes:

- **Week 1** — Overview of spirituality and health applied to OT. This included time for reflection about what the students would hope to learn from the module, as well as having time to share each other's personal beliefs and values about spirituality (Townsend *et al*, 1999; Kirsch *et al*, 2001). The students were encouraged to use reflective tools such as: SWOB analysis, reflective diaries, and personal significant event records (Hong and Harrison, 2004).
- **Week 2** — Exploration of definitions about spirituality with an emphasis on the need to consider and respect diverse beliefs about spirituality (Johnston and Mayers, 2005), emphasising that no single definition is conclusive (Collins, 2006).
- **Week 3** — Examination of the relationship between spiritual assessment (McLaughlin, 2004) and therapeutic use of self (Collins, 2007a). This session provided opportunities for students to practise spiritual assessments on each other (in pairs) with a group discussion (Koenig, 2004).
- **Week 4** — Opportunity to reflect on personal and professional development, using focused inner work exercises to facilitate awareness of the personal shadow[1] as formulated by analytical psychologist Carl Jung (Collins, 2007a).
- **Week 5** — Exploration of the interface between spirituality, human occupation and transpersonal[2] developments (Collins, 2008, 2010), which

---

[1]The shadow represents unconscious and unacknowledged processes that can be projected onto others, which are often prejudicial.

[2]Transpersonal states of consciousness go beyond everyday ego-identification, and are typically experienced as a deeper universal connection to life, or a greater sense of belonging with others, including animals, nature and the planet/cosmos as a whole.

included discussions on the role and function of human occupation in the management of spiritual crisis (Collins, 2007b).

- **Week 6** — Review and reflection of personal and group learning, which allowed time to identify further learning and CPD (Hong and Harrison, 2004).

I was mindful that creating a dynamic learning environment raises the possibility that students could encounter deep learning experiences, which may include intrinsic motivation, experimental learning, personal development, as well as the explicit use of reflection (Ashcroft and Foreman-Peck, 1994). The students' reflections (outlined below) have revealed important information concerning the educational processes associated with learning about spirituality in two ways. First, the students have demonstrated that engaging spirituality in the OT curriculum can be productive in terms of them becoming proactive in the various ways that they learn about spirituality. Second, the students' reflections and evaluations have played an important role in understanding how students' learning experiences connected – to a greater or lesser extent – to their personal and professional sense of self. The students' experiences have echoed the reflective proposition put forward by Ghaye (2004) who has asserted that 'spiritual practice embraces an awareness and appreciation of self and others and a capacity to respond to the other in ways that nourish significant life meaning'.

The educator's reflective process

The third year students from two cohorts in 2007 (7 students) and 2008 (10 students) chose to attend the six week spirituality module from a list of other course options. Students had diverse backgrounds in terms of spiritual orientation including some participants coming from different religious/cultural backgrounds, who wanted to find out more about spirituality and how it links to their chosen profession. Some students identified themselves as non-spiritual or non-religious, but were curious to find out more, whilst other students were drawn to the module due to their interests in new forms of spiritual expression, such as those practices associated with holistic and complementary healing. The module was developed in accordance with the College of Occupational Therapists' *Code of ethics and professional conduct* (2010) and the Health Professions Council (2003) *Standards of proficiency for occupational therapists*.

My aspirations as a facilitator of this module were based on providing rich learning opportunities as well as essential resources for the students (Bee and Bee, 1998). Moreover, I was interested in being present to my own transpersonal and spiritual reflections that are connected to a grounded transpersonal self, which according to Mayes (2001) can 'become more observant, more responsive, more authentically caring – in short, more nurturing to our students'. My experience of running this module over two years made me mindful of my own attitudes, values, beliefs, and behaviours within the learning environment. The students' evaluations of the six week modules were gathered using anonymous questionnaires, which asked them to comment on each of the sessions. This type of module feedback does not constitute formal research, however, the module feedback has reflected the students' authentic engagement with the learning process, and highlighted interesting areas to explore further through research. The student feedback will be discussed in the three broad themes mentioned above: (1) reflection with others, (2) reflection on self, and (3) reflection on practice.

Student feedback

Reflection with others

During the planning stage for the module development I had considered that the first session needed to take account of the fact that the group would take time to form. Therefore the emphasis was placed on a general introduction about spirituality as well creating time to express personal interests and expectations about the course. Student feedback was positive about the intentions behind the course structure:

> *...was good to have an overview of what was coming, and also have some input in how it can shape our practice by stating our needs and expectations of the course.*
> (Student 6: 08).

The students in both groups appeared to engage authentically from the outset. It was anticipated that an important part of this module would be working with and sharing reflections about spirituality with each other; therefore this intention was made explicit in the first sessions. The following comment reflects the importance of this in terms of the quality of students' discussions:

> *I felt that people were able to share things on a more personal level. This session started a very useful conversation with another group member that helped my spiritual development.*
> (Student 2: 07).

143

Gaining a sense of group cohesion and trust appeared to be helpful in preparing the students to work productively in pairs, as well as having regular opportunities for feedback and reflection within the larger group, which appeared to facilitate a willingness to experiment. For example, the students were given the opportunity to practise spiritual assessments on each other. The two spiritual assessments used were (1) FICA: faith, importance, community and address and (2) HOPE: hope, organised religion, personal practices and end-of-life issues (McLaughlin, 2004). The students' reflections confirmed that they found using spiritual assessments a useful exercise:

> *For me, learning about the assessments and being able to have a go has been a big learning experience.*
>
> (Student 7: 07).
>
> *The chance to practise using the assessments on each other helped to translate what we had been learning into a usable form of practice.*
>
> (Student 3: 08).

The process of opening up to each other involved taking risks when practising assessments on each other, which included sharing personal beliefs, values, experiences, and perceptions about spirituality:

> *Assessments are actually out there! – by doing work in pairs it made me think about myself and how difficult it can be for the therapist and the client.*
>
> (Student 10: 07).

The dynamics of working closely and being open with each other appeared to create an experiential approach in both of the groups, which was underpinned by a respect for one another's beliefs. However, the students had to negotiate the complexities of discussing issues that were deeply personal – and initially – not easy to share:

> *I did find knowing the boundaries difficult as spirituality can be a touchy subject if people's views are entirely different, but I felt the group was respectful.*
>
> (Student 3: 07).

It appeared as if the process of sharing personal information with each other also created a learning environment that was initially challenging, but became more empowered when the students' confidence grew:

It was good to feel that you could express your own opinions but this felt challenging and uncomfortable.
(Student 6: 07).

The quality of group cohesion between the students in both of the modules appeared to have added another dimension to the students' learning experiences, which was centred on being personally engaged in productive conversations and shared reflections:

I now feel I would be able to introduce spirituality into conversations with colleagues to find out their views, and if it is something they include or avoid when working with patients.
(Student 1: 07).

Reflection on self

The gradual exposure to the deeper issues connected to spirituality, including sharing personal beliefs, as well as the group members' active engagement when reflecting with one another, appeared to create an environment that encouraged authentic self-reflection:

Exploring spirituality has given me an opportunity to consider things about myself that may have otherwise been neglected.
(Student 1: 07).
It increased my interest [...] and allowed me to discuss and explore spirituality before addressing it with future clients.
(Student 1: 07).

The students appeared willing to take the opportunity to explore their personal experiences in much greater depth than I had initially anticipated. This was particularly evident in the session on spirituality and the personal shadow, which provided opportunities for students to self-reflect on areas of personal experience that had not previously been considered in their professional education:

This session was essential as it made me think about integrating spirituality into practice and what problems and prejudices we may come across. It has encouraged me to reflect on my beliefs and how to manage them professionally.
(Student 4: 07).

145

> *By being introduced to the concept of the shadow I am now more aware that we all have some prejudices – but by being aware of these we are able to work more efficiently with patients by respecting their views and not imposing our own.*
>
> (Student 1: 07).

The session on the shadow confronted the students with their attitudes and beliefs, which could potentially influence their perceptions of other people's spirituality. However, the emphasis of the session at the outset was focused on developing self-awareness and not to generate critical judgements towards self or others. The groups found this session difficult, and 'challenging' (Student 6: 08); however, they worked productively:

> *I am biased when it comes to others' spiritual beliefs, sometimes without realising it.*
>
> (Student 1: 08).
>
> *Discussing spirituality and the shadow really made me think about my own views and prejudices and how I would deal with them in practice.*
>
> (Student 8: 07).

The positive benefits of exploring the personal shadow were identified:

> *For me, this session really highlighted how important it is to reflect when using spirituality to prevent prejudices and be aware of my own shadow.*
>
> (Student 7: 07).
>
> *I examined an intervention with a patient on my caseload during a palliative care placement, and it made me realise that I had projected something from my personal shadow initially, which hindered my rapport with the patient for a short time, although I did manage to rectify this.*
>
> (Student 6: 08).

From the outset the modules emphasised the importance of self-reflection, and it appeared from the feedback that many of the students found this a stimulating process to engage in. Moreover, the comments from the students have highlighted the positive relationship of understanding their own spirituality as an important step towards understanding other people's spiritual values, beliefs, and behaviours. There were many examples of how students benefited from exploring the boundaries between their personal and professional sense of self:

> *The word spirituality opens up a whole new world – I'm starting to explore and find myself. I am making changes in my life that I never thought I would, and it has made*

146

me understand myself a lot better – probably wouldn't have done so if it wasn't for these sessions. It just helps when everyone is learning and understanding.
(Student 9: 07).

The session we were given to take time out and reflect was really helpful, as we don't often get given/take time to think and reflect. I have spent time really critically reflecting on myself and my own spirituality.
(Student 3: 08).

The opportunity for self-reflection was not a comfortable experience for many of the students, which gives some indication that they had engaged deeply and authentically with their own learning and reflections. Exploring the boundaries between the personal and the professional spheres of self was challenging and at times 'overwhelming' for some students:

I found it hard to look at my own spirituality and feel that this has changed due to studying, and that I need to regain these things to be me again. At times I felt very vulnerable and lost and frustrated.
(Student 6: 07).

At times I've been a bit confused and felt things are a bit deep and over my head, but good things have come from this and I feel more confident to address spirituality personally and professionally.
(Student 2: 07).

Reflection on practice

It is evident that the module enabled the students to make connections between the theories on spirituality and their future practice. The student feedback was encouraging and I was particularly interested to note how the students were willing to engage both personal and professional issues surrounding spirituality. The students revealed that reflections on self and reflections with others played an important role in developing awareness and the confidence to integrate spirituality into practice:

The module has made me much more aware of clients' potential spiritual needs and how I can address those. I am still a little unsure/apprehensive to really use it in practice.
(Student 5: 08).

It has encouraged me to become more reflective about how I can develop professionally. It has made me aware that even though I don't have any religious

147

or spiritual beliefs, it may come up in clinical practice, and being reflective can help me deal with these issues.

(Student 4: 07).

In terms of professional practice the module prompted some of the students to consider the link between spirituality and client-centred practice:

It made me feel able to address spirituality... as it introduced me to a variety of ways of bringing the subject up.

(Student 1: 07).

The students were also exposed to new knowledge and how a transpersonal perspective could be considered in relation to future practice developments. This sparked lively discussions in both groups, which appeared to engender a desire for further study and learning about how spirituality can be linked to the engagement and expression of human health and potential, for example:

I discovered that there is an official term 'transpersonal experiences' for those moments of connectedness.

(Student 2: 07).

Many of the students clearly embodied the notion that engagement of spirituality not only requires self-reflection to manage the boundaries between the personal–professional dimensions of self, but also how their spiritual beliefs and values can promote their growth and development as professionals and human beings:

It has made me re-engage with my personal thinking and beliefs and made me realise how I use my spirituality unconsciously in a lot of my practice already. Therefore, if I consciously use it, then it will be more effective.

(Student 6: 08).
I realise that my spirituality is very much a part of who I am, and that I need to acknowledge this and use it positively (therapeutic use of self).

(Student 6: 08).

Reflection on the modules

The students' reflections on the modules revealed how they used the learning opportunities that were designed for personal–professional reflection, illustrating that this may be an important area for further development. Addressing personal responses to spirituality appeared to enable professional reflection, for example, the following comment by one of the students illustrates an authentic response revealing new insights that linked personal and professional spheres of self:

> *Reflection has also allowed me to address possible prejudices that, had they been undetected, may have impacted on my practice.*
>
> (Student 1: 07).

The opportunity to use structured reflective tools within the sessions was considered a useful way of engaging with the personal–professional influences on spirituality. Moreover, reflective engagement in the modules was aimed at facilitating the students to gain awareness of how personal influences may impact on professional practice.

However, this exploration was initiated through each student deciding how far he or she wanted to explore such issues, not through external authority or expectations from others:

> *I see part of my CPD in the future to involve continually reflecting on my beliefs and of course others' beliefs [...] seeing a person as a whole.*
>
> (Student 4: 07).
>
> *It has made me a lot more aware of my own spiritual needs and also my strengths and weaknesses.*
>
> (Student 5: 08).

There was a clear sense that the modules had impacted on the students' learning, which appeared to engage their genuine interest in the subject:

> *I enjoyed going deeper with my reflections, this aspect of the course facilitated me to do that.*
>
> (Student 5: 08)

I had designed the modules to give students opportunities for learning and reflection on spirituality, which is an area of practice that is recognised as being difficult to address. The students' feedback highlighted an important issue; that is, one possible reason why spirituality is avoided could be as much to do with the personal–professional divide, as it is with a theory–practice gap, as noted by Belcham (2004):

I definitely feel more confident in bringing up spirituality with patients...previously this has been a taboo area.

(Student 2: 07).

It bridged the gap between theory and practice.

(Student 3: 08).

Engaging spirituality through therapeutic use of self

A key area for integrating spirituality into therapeutic practice is through therapeutic use of self (Collins, 2007a), which encompasses both personal and professional dimensions. The reflective exercise below is a method for encouraging the integration of spirituality into practice through therapeutic use of self and CPD:

• Find a mentor or peer group who would be interested in exploring the links between spirituality and therapeutic use of self with you
• Carry out an individual SWOB (strengths, weaknesses, opportunities or barriers) analysis in relation to engaging spirituality through therapeutic use of self
• Explore your responses to the SWOB analysis (above) and select one area on which to focus further
• Once you have considered the issue identified formulate a reflective question about that issue, for example, 'How can I engage more compassionately in my therapeutic practice? Make sure that the question has a specific focus
• Let the above question guide your CPD for a set period, e.g., for two months. During this time: (1) Capture a range of different development scenarios connected to your question) using significant event records, e.g., positive, negative, theoretical, or conceptual, etc. (2) Keep a diary record of (pithy) accounts that reflect any qualitative shifts and developments, or complexities that you are encountering. (3) Share any significant developments or difficulties with your mentor or peer group. Keep a record of these meetings
• At the end of the two months carry out another SWOB analysis and reflect on any change or development.

The value of reflecting on spirituality and therapeutic use of self is conveyed by transpersonal psychologist Amy Mindell (1995) when she suggests that the practice of therapy can provide therapists with opportunities to develop their spiritual capacities. Indeed, some of the students' reflections echoed this sentiment:

[It] helped me explore my own spirituality and understand self – need to know where we are at, in order to help others.

(Student 9: 07).

It has been challenging to look at ourselves...I feel I need to learn and discover more about myself, and that this is a long journey.

(Student 6: 07).

The interface between spirituality and therapists' use of self can be a potent area for therapists' practice and development (Rowan and Jacobs, 2002. Wosket, 1999), as the following students discovered:

I have spent a lot of time over the weeks with some kind of debate/thought process about spirituality going on in my head, especially regarding the upcoming elective placement.

(Student 2: 08).

I actually wanted to read articles for interest and this encouraged conversation with colleagues about future innovations and the word spirituality.

(Student 6: 07).

Conclusion

Preparing and delivering this module to occupational therapy students who had no previous experience of working with spirituality on practice placements provided me with some valuable insights into the structure and processes linked to professional education and reflection. The student evaluations have revealed a level of authentic engagement with the subject that was entirely driven by the connections that they were making between their personal and professional interests, which then linked to theory–practice considerations. The students' willingness to share personal and professional issues with each other in an environment of openness and honesty appeared to add a vital ingredient into the learning environment.

My reflections about this module have been stimulated by the students' authentic engagement in the reflective process. Whilst it is important to emphasise the need to reduce the theory–practice gap through training and education, it is also important to consider the dynamic interactions between the personal and the professional spheres of influence. The interface between personal and professional reflections may be challenging – as noted in the students' feedback – but it also appears to encourage students to gain a deep and meaningful experience of the importance of spirituality to health and well-being. I shall let the following student quotation speak for the level of personal and professional reflection that was often present within the groups:

> *[There were] many opportunities for critical reflection, as so many questions/ thoughts arose.*
>
> (Student 2: 08).

Key points

- Reflections that are focused on self, with others, and on practice are important for developing spirituality within the education and training of health professionals
- Reflection that acknowledges the relationship between complex areas of practice, such as spirituality and the shadow could be productive in terms of engaging deeper levels of self-awareness and an appreciation of the diverse ways that spirituality may be expressed
- Reflection between spirituality and the personal and professional spheres of self appear to be an important link that helps to prepare students to integrate theory into therapeutic practice

References

Ashcroft K, Foreman-Peck L (1994) *Managing teaching and learning in further and higher education.* Routledge Falmer Press, London

Barry E, Gibbens R (2011) Spirituality in practice: Using personal reflection to prepare occupational therapy students. *British Journal of Occupational Therapy* **74**(4): 176–80

Bee F, Bee R (1998) *Facilitation skills.* Institute of Personnel and Development, London

Belcham C (2004) Spirituality in occupational therapy: Theory in practice? *British Journal of Occupational Therapy* **67**(1): 39–46

Boden M (1990) *The creative mind: Myths and mechanisms.* Weidenfeld and Nicholson, London

Boyd EM, Fales AW (1983) Reflective learning: Key to learning from experience. *Journal of Humanistic Psychology* **23**(2): 99–117

Brew A (2006) *Research and teaching: Beyond the divide.* Palgrave Macmillan, Basingstoke

Bulpitt H, Martin P (2005) Learning about reflection from the student. *Learning in Higher Education* **6**(3): 207–17

Cannon R, Newble D (2000) *A handbook for teaching in universities and colleges: A guide to improving teaching methods.* Kogan Page Limited, London

Christiansen C (1997) Acknowledging the spiritual dimension in occupational therapy practice. *American Journal of Occupational Therapy* **51**(3): 169–80

College of Occupational Therapists (2010) *Code of ethics and professional conduct.* COT, London:

Collins M (1998) Occupational therapy and spirituality: Reflecting on quality of experience in therapeutic interventions. *British Journal of Occupational Therapy* **61**(6): 280–4

Collins M (2001) Who is occupied? Consciousness, self-awareness and the process of human adaptation. *Journal of Occupational Science* **8**(1): 25–32

Collins M (2006) Unfolding spirituality: Working with and beyond definitions. *International Journal of Therapy and Rehabilitation* **13**(6): 254–8

Collins M (2007a) Spirituality and the shadow: Reflection and the therapeutic use of self. *British Journal of Occupational Therapy* **70**(2): 88–90

Collins M (2007b) Spiritual emergency and occupational identity: A transpersonal perspective. *British Journal of Occupational Therapy* **70**(12): 504–12

Collins M (2008) Transpersonal identity and human occupation. *British Journal of Occupational Therapy* **71**(12): 549–52

Collins M (2010) Engaging transcendent actualisation through occupational intelligence. *Journal of Occupational Science* **17**(3): 177–86

Cottrell S (2003) *Skills for success: The personal development planning book.* Palgrave MacMillan, Basingstoke

Cowley S (2005) *Letting the buggers be creative.* Continuum International Publishing Group, London

Cranton P, Carusetta E (2004) Perspectives on authenticity in teaching. *Adult Education Quarterly* **55**(1): 5–22

Csontó S (2009) Occupational therapy students' consideration of clients' spirituality in practice placement education. *British Journal of Occupational Therapy* **72**(10): 442–9

Culliford L (2002) Spirituality and clinical care. *British Medical Journal* **325:** 1434–5

Daaleman T, Kuckelman-Cobb A, Frey B (2001) Spirituality and well-being: An exploratory study of the patient perspective. *Social Science and Medicine* **53**(11): 1053–511

Delega VJ, Metts S, Petronio S, Margulis ST (1993) *Self-disclosure.* Sage Publications, Newbury Park, CA

Department of Health (2000) *Meeting the challenge: A strategy for the allied health professions.* NHS Executive, London

Department of Health (2004) *Standards for better health.* NHS Executive, London

do Rozario L (1997) Spirituality in the lives of people with disability and chronic illness: A creative paradigm of wholeness and reconstitution. *Disability and Rehabilitation* **19**(10): 427–34

Egan M, De Laat D (1994) Considering spirituality in occupational therapy practice. *Canadian Journal of Occupational Therapy* **61**(2): 95–101

Ghaye T (2004) Editorial: Reflection for spiritual practice. *Reflective Practice* **5**(3): 291–5

Health Professions Council (2003) *Standards of proficiency for occupational therapists.* HPC, London

Hobbs H (2007) Faking it or hating it: Can reflective practice be forced? *Reflective Practice* **8**(3): 405–17

Hollis J (2000) *Creating a life: Finding your individual path.* Inner City Books, Toronto

Hong CS, Harrison D eds (2004) *Tools for continuing professional development.* Quay Books, Dinton, Wilts

Jarvis M (2005) *The psychology of effective learning and teaching.* Nelson Thornes Limited, Cheltenham

Johnston D, Mayers C (2005) Spirituality: A review of how occupational therapists acknowledge, assess and meet spiritual needs. *British Journal of Occupational Therapy* **68**(9): 386–92

Kang C (2003) A psychospiritual integration frame of reference for occupational therapy. Part 1: Conceptual foundations. *Australian Journal of Occupational Therapy* **50:** 92–103

Kirsch B, Dawson D, Antolikova S, Reynolds L (2001) Developing awareness of spirituality in occupational therapy students: Are our curricula up to the task? *Occupational Therapy International* **8**(2): 119–25

Koenig H (2004) Taking a spiritual history. *Journal of the American Medical Association* **291**(23): 2881

Kolb D (1984) *Experiential learning.* Prentice Hall, Hemel Hempstead:

Kottler J (1986) *On being a therapist.* Jossey-Bass, San Francisco

Mayes C (2001) A transpersonal model for teacher reflectivity. *Journal of Curriculum Studies* **33**(4): 477–93

McColl MA, Bickenbach J, Johnston J, Nishihama S, Schumaker M, Smith K, Smith M, Yealland B (2000) Spiritual issues associated with traumatic onset disability. *Disability and Rehabilitation* **22**(12): 555–64

McLaughlin D (2004) Incorporating individual spiritual beliefs in treatment of inpatient mental health consumers. *Perspectives in Psychiatric Care* **40**(3): 114–9

Mindell A (1995) *Metaskills: The spiritual art of therapy* New Falcon Publications, Tempe

Moon J (2000) *Reflection in learning and professional development* Kogan Page Ltd, London

Pain H (2005) Letter: Spirituality. *British Journal of Occupational Therapy* **68**(12): 583

Ponton M, Derrick M, Carr P (2005) The relationship between resourcefulness and persistence in adult autonomous learning. *Adult Education Quarterly* **55**(2): 116–28

Ramsden P (2003) *Learning to teach in higher education.* 2nd edn. Routledge Falmer, London

Regan P (2008) Reflective practice: How far, how deep? *Reflective Practice* **9**(2): 210–29

Rowan J, Jacobs M (2002) *The therapist's use of self.* Open University Press, Buckingham

Schön D (1987) *Educating the reflective practitioner.* Jossey Bass, San Francisco, CA

Schulz EK (2005) The meaning of spirituality for individuals with disabilities. *Disability and Rehabilitation* **27**(21): 1283–95

Townsend E, De Laat D, Egan M, Thibeault R, Alan Wright W (1999) *Spirituality in enabling occupation: A learner centred workbook.* CAOT Publications ACE, Ottawa, Ontario

Unruh A, Versnal J, Kerr N (2002) Spirituality unplugged: A review of commonalities and contentions and a resolution. *Canadian Journal of Occupational Therapy* **69**(1): 5–19

Whipp M (1998) Spirituality and the scientific mind. In: Cobb M, Robshaw V eds. *The spiritual challenge of health care.* Churchill Livingstone, Edinburgh

Wilson L (2010) Spirituality, occupation and occupational therapy revisited: Ongoing consideration of the issues for occupational therapists. *British Journal of Occupational Therapy* **73**(9): 437–40

Wosket V (1999) *The therapeutic use of self: Counselling practice, research and supervision.* Routledge, London

Wright S (1998) The reflective journey begins a spiritual journey. In: Johns C, Freshwater D eds. *Transforming nursing through reflective practice.* Blackwell Science, Oxford

Chapter 12

Service improvement tools for CPD

Introduction

Jon Larner and Julie Collier

Over the past decade successive Governments have worked hard to drive up the quality of healthcare provision in the NHS. New ways of measuring quality have been introduced that underpin performance management, and patient satisfaction is now considered to be one of the most important benchmarks of success. The economic pressures on public funding have made it necessary to find ways of saving money whilst maintaining or improving the quality of care we provide. It is possible to improve the quality and safety of healthcare, to make working lives less stressful for staff and to boost productivity, without a large injection of funding. This impressive goal can be achieved by applying some tried and tested methodology for service improvement. This does not require years of experience, in fact a fresh pair of eyes can be particularly helpful when applying these principles (Adair, 2009).

There are many tools available to assist with improving the pathway for service users and it is important not to become overwhelmed by the terminology used to describe service improvement. The concept is relatively straightforward and simple to apply in practice. This chapter focuses on two important tools:

* Process mapping for identifying where improvements can be made
* The PDSA (Plan, Do, Study, Act) cycle for developing a framework to enable the outcome of process mapping to be translated into action.

What is service improvement about?

* Making the outcomes of healthcare interventions better and safer for patients and their families
* Increasing the quality and value of healthcare
* Improving the efficiency of our work

- Making it easier for staff to do their job effectively by improving systems and processes.

A helpful way to view improvement is to think of it as a discipline that involves four equally important and inter-related parts that are seen by many to be the foundation for all improvement activities. See *Figure 12.1.*

Who should be involved in service improvement?

Whilst the desire to want to improve often comes predominantly from an individual, changes that carry the biggest impact are usually those that have engaged the whole team of people involved. As it is rare in healthcare for a patient's journey to involve only a single practitioner, or in fact a single profession, it is vital to involve everyone in the process of change. Wherever possible the thoughts and opinions of the service-users should be sought and included in the discussion. Even though it might be an individual who recognises the need for change or has the initial idea, improvement projects should be team-focused to ensure that any improvements can be successfully built into daily work. Ultimately, it is desirable to develop a culture of continual improvement within a team or organisation and

Figure 12.1. The four parts of the discipline of improvement (Penny, 2003).

to achieve this it is critical to include everyone in the process. Without this level of shared involvement it is difficult to influence behaviour in a way that will make improvements sustainable over time.

Where should I start when making a service improvement?

Often we are aware that something needs to change, but we are not really clear about exactly what is causing the problem, or what to do about it. Unless a simple solution is immediately obvious it is usually best to analyse the situation carefully, rather than leaping straight from the problem to a solution. This will help minimise the risk of jumping to the wrong conclusion or over-simplifying the situation. Process mapping is a helpful tool for doing this and we will take a look at this shortly. However, first it is important to have an overarching framework for developing, testing and implementing any changes that might lead to improvement. The model devised by Langley *et al* (1996) has been widely used in healthcare and is recommended by the NHS Improvement Faculty.

A model for improvement: The PDSA cycle

Langley *et al*'s model (1996) includes three key questions that every person should ask before starting an improvement project (see *Figure 12.2*). It has a clear process for testing the change idea using a four-stage cycle known as a Plan, Do, Study, Act (PDSA) cycle.

- **Plan** — Having asked themselves the three questions outlined in the model, the team should analyse the current situation carefully in order to try and identify where appropriate improvements can be made. This can be done by using a process mapping tool which is discussed later. From this analysis it is sensible to identify a small desirable change to implement. In reality small 'bite-size' chunks of change are the most effective
- **Do** — The small change is implemented and the effects are measured
- **Study** — The effect of the change is discussed by the group with reflection on the outcomes. Decisions are made regarding the best way forward
- **Act** — The group acts upon these decisions and implements permanent change as appropriate.

159

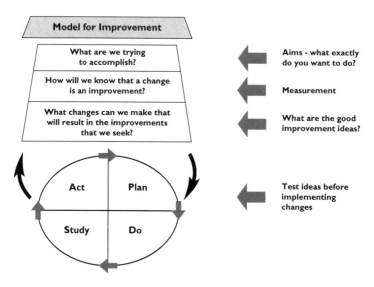

Figure 12.2. A model for improvement – From Langley et al (1996).

Why use the PDSA cycle?

- To test or adapt a change idea, to try it out as a pilot
- To implement a change
- To spread the changes to the rest of your system.

Why test things out as a pilot?

- To increase the belief that your change will result in improvement
- To predict how much improvement can be expected from your change
- To learn how to adapt the change to conditions in the local environment
- To evaluate costs and side-effects of your change
- To minimise resistance upon implementation.

Using successive cycles to test change

In reality successful implementation of change often involves a series of successive PDSA cycles that follow naturally from each other. Each PDSA cycle will highlight a series of actions that can be progressively refined until the desired outcome is achieved. There are a number of tips for managing this change model:

- Plan multiple cycles to test your change
- Think a couple of cycles ahead
- Keep the size of your change as small as possible (number of patients, locations etc.)
- Test it with volunteers
- Although you need to involve the team, do not try to get buy-in and consensus from everyone
- Be innovative to make your test feasible
- Collect useful data during each test
- Test your change over a wide range of conditions.

Why measure the outcomes?

Measuring outcomes allows us to move away from anecdotal evidence to focusing on objective data. It helps us to follow a process accurately over time and clearly see the effects of changes. It can also help to increase the understanding of where there is variation between the processes. An example of this is where patients are not receiving the same treatment for a particular condition. This could be because national guidelines have not been used or maybe because the referral system is not consistent (not all patients are accessing services in a timely manner). Alternatively, patients may have been referred to the wrong service which results in a rather long-winded route to the right place. For example, in different parts of a county some GPs may have their own individual referral form without clear criteria. Hospitals will accept the referral even though they do not think it is appropriate and then try to find a suitable department for the patient to be referred to. The process puts patients at risk of delayed diagnosis and treatment.

Using a process map to analyse the current situation

We have established that it is important to use a structured service improvement model to test out our change ideas and implement improvements. However, once we have identified an area for improvement, it can sometimes be difficult to know where to start or where the problems are with the current situation. A process map is a really useful tool for establishing a clear picture of what is happening and is therefore helpful for signposting where improvements can be made (NHSI, 2007).

What is process mapping?

A process is a series of connected steps with a start and an end point; mapping is an exercise to identify all the steps in the process.

Process mapping is a simple exercise. It helps a team to know where to start making improvements that will have the biggest impact for patients and staff. More information can be found at www.modern.nhs.uk/improvementguides

A process map is a picture. Just as a road map is a picture of how you get from A to B, a process map is a picture of the patient's journey through your process. It could also be a picture of how a specific transaction travels through your process, for example the journey that a purchase order takes from first contact with the supplier to payment of invoice. The map shows all of the steps in a process. The reason we use a road map rather than a narrative description of how to get from A to B is obvious – we would get hopelessly lost otherwise. We use a process map for the same reason.

Why map a process in healthcare?

The first step is to draw a flow diagram, then everyone understands what his job is. If people do not see the process, they cannot improve it.
WE Deming (cited in Arora and Johnson, 2006)

• It helps you to see healthcare from everyone's point of view
• It gives you a picture of the whole process of care
• It creates an opportunity for all staff involved in patient care to work together
• It gives the opportunity to pool ideas
• It helps inform the baseline (where we are now)
• You can clearly identify problems, e.g. show how many times a patient has to wait or how many steps there are to access care
• It helps to identify gaps and provides potential for improving the service.

How do I map a process?

We want to get the simplest possible picture of how the process works, and simple is the key word here. The aim of process mapping is to make things clear – to provide us with insight, and the best map is the simplest map that provides that insight. It is therefore very important to have a sense of proportion with respect to process mapping. You do not need to go on a day's workshop to learn how to draw boxes and diamonds. Doing a process map is straightforward. It is the questions that you ask as you are mapping and what happens after mapping that matter.

The people who work in the process should do the mapping. It is advisable to:

- Be open and honest about the current process. Always map what actually happens in the current process rather than what you would like to be happening, or what should be happening according to the book
- Involve all disciplines and all levels of staff. If you have a ward clerk or receptionist in your department, make sure he or she is involved
- It is may also be useful to draw a picture of the ideal process. If you were starting with a blank piece of paper and there were no constraints, how would you design this process? This will be useful later when you start to improve the service and it is interesting to compare it with this ideal
- When you first start to map a process draw the 'big picture' first, i.e. a very high level map of the whole process on a single piece of paper, to give yourself a good feel for what you are looking at
- Before you start make sure you have defined the boundaries of the process you have chosen to look at, i.e. where does it start and end? It is important to be quite clear on what you are *not* looking at.

A set of post-it notes and a pen are the main resources you need. It is important to have enough space to work in and to post the notes. From this point you can brainstorm each part of the process, adding and changing post-its as the discussion progresses. With a visual representation of the process in front of you it is easier to identify parts of the map where there are problems, for example bottlenecks or delays, and you will also be able to see parts of the process where there are lots of steps involved.

Although the process map is an essential part of your toolkit, it is not about learning what lots of different shapes and symbols mean. It is not about drawing fancy, computer-generated pictures. It is simply insight that we are after. Look at the example of an anticoagulant blood testing process carried out in a major hospital in *Figure 12.3*.

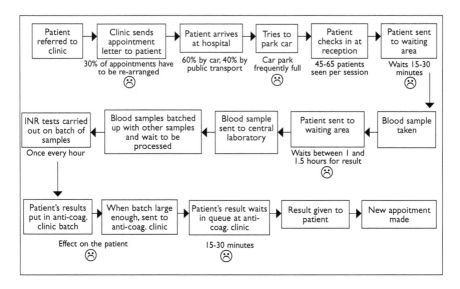

Figure 12.3. The anticoagulant blood testing process.

From the map you can see where the process affects the patient in a negative way and where there are delays. Delays could be due to many reasons, and that is why when it is mapped like this you can question in a systematic way. The following gives some helpful tips for effective mapping:

- Do not map everything. When some people find out about process mapping they spend the next two years mapping every process in their organisation. Only map the process that you have chosen to improve
- Let your process map cross functional boundaries. For example, if you are looking at a referral or discharge process, you want to see the whole, end-to-end process, not just the piece of the process inside your department. Improving one department or section does not always improve a service that flows through several departments. It is always much more important to manage the interactions between departments than it is to manage the actions inside each.

How can I use my process map?

Your process map will give you insight into the situation. It may highlight a number of obvious problems that could be addressed, such as:

164

Simplifying the process

- Removing steps that are not necessary
- Making the process easier to follow.

Standardising the process

- Reducing variation — For example: If a patient has chest pain, the standard process for all patients is to dial 999, not ring their GP or NHS Direct or community services. This means that all patients will be assessed by a paramedic and transported to hospital following nationally agreed guidelines and protocols
- Understanding when steps do not apply — Using the example above, if a patient rings the GP, this may prompt a home visit before ringing 999, putting an extra time-consuming step into the process
- Investigating quickly when a step is not used — This can be done by regularly reviewing patient notes for any evidence that they have received a timely response. This can be undertaken until the rate of inconsistency is reduced and everyone agrees that all steps have been taken to eliminate inconsistencies.

The following questions may act as prompts when evaluating your process map. They may help you to recognise typical areas where improvements could be made:

- How many times is the service-user passed from one person to another (known as a hand off)?
- Where are delays or queues built into the process?
- Where are the bottlenecks?
- What are the longest delays?
- What is the approximate time taken for each step (task time)?
- What is the approximate time between each step (wait time)?
- What is the approximate time between the first and last step?
- How many steps are there for the service-user?
- How many steps add no value for the service-user?
- Are there things that are done more than once?
- Can you see any reworked loops, where work is unnecessarily delayed waiting for something else to happen?
- Is work being batched (stored until there are sufficient numbers to proceed)?

- Where are the problems for the service-user?
- At each step, is the action being undertaken by the most appropriate staff member?
- Where are the problems for staff?
- Where is the greatest amount of time currently lost or wasted?
- Can any processes be carried out simultaneously?
- Consider what service-users complain about
- Are any other teams affected if your team changes its process.

How can I document service improvement for my CPD portfolio?

Being able to show that you have engaged with service improvement is valuable evidence of CPD. Process maps that have been produced with your team provide a clear record of the outcome of the analysis, but the learning becomes even clearer when it is coupled with reflections on your experience. The template in *Figure 12.4* is used by allied health profession students at the University of East Anglia for reflecting on their improvement projects. The template starts with the three issues that should be addressed at the start of every improvement project, namely background, actions and improvement measurement (Langley *et al*, 1996). It then prompts you to reflect formally on your improvement project.

The list of questions in the template is not exhaustive but will act as a prompt to encourage formal reflection on the event as a learning experience. Finally the template prompts you to append your process map as evidence of your analysis.

Summary

The following seven steps summarise the service improvement framework:

Step 1 Define the aim for the project including:
- The group of patients you are considering
- What you want to achieve – your own targets

Step 2 Consider how you are going to know if a change is an improvement:
- What measures are you going to use?
- How you are going to report progress to all interested parties?

Service improvement template
Background — This should include your aim (what you are trying to accomplish). Description of problem and your identification of the need for improvement including any implications for patients, carers and staff
Actions — What changes can you make that will result in the improvement you seek? The steps you plan to take or have taken to address the need for improvement including stakeholder/colleague involvement and specific activities/actions
Impact measurement – How will you know that a change is an improvement? The change your improvement activities should make or have made for patients, carers, staff or a service including any specific indicators or measures of that change
Reflection
What went well?
Who did you involve? (patient/user/colleague/MDT)
Did the improvement link to any current improvement programmes in your placement setting?
Were there any issues/constraints?
Did the team agree to take your ideas forward?
Have you appended your process map?

Figure 12.4: Service improvement template used at the School of AHP, UEA.

Step 3   Involve the staff in mapping and analysing the process:
- Really understand the problems for patients, their carers and staff
- Start to measure and create the baselines for your improvements. You may need to revisit your targets at this point

Step 4   Investigate all the changes that are likely to make an improvement in line with the aims set:
- Talk to other healthcare services, organisations and the patients
- Look at helpful resources such as Improvement Leaders Guides

Step 5   Test out the change ideas to see if they actually do make improvements:
  • Consider the knock-on effects that making one change will have to that process and other parts of the system or different systems
Step 6   Implement the change that will make improvements
Step 7   Congratulate the team and celebrate your success but continue to:
  • Revise often to ensure the improvements are sustained and the new improved process is still fit for purpose
  • Look for ways to continue to improve
  • Offer help, advice and support to other improvement teams

Key points

• Although an individual may recognise the need to initiate a change, improvement should be a team activity
• It is helpful to ask three questions before starting an improvement project (Langley, 1996):
  - What are we trying to accomplish?
  - How do we know that a change is an improvement?
  - What changes can we make that will result in the improvements that we seek?
• The Plan, Do, Study, Act (PDSA) cycle provides a clear process for testing your change idea
• Measuring outcomes allows us to move away from anecdotal evidence to focusing on objective data
• A process map is a really useful and simple tool for establishing a clear picture of what is currently happening, it therefore signposts where improvements can be made
• Process mapping should ideally involve the whole team of people responsible for the process being analysed. It should provide an open and honest picture of what is actually happening, not what should ideally be happening
• Once completed a process map will provide insight into the situation and should highlight obvious problems or opportunities to simplify or standardise the process
• Don't forget to celebrate your successes and congratulate the whole team

References

Adair J (2009) *Effective innovation: The essential guide to staying ahead of the competition.* New Revised Edition. Pan Books, London

Arora V, Johnson J (2006) National Patient Safety Goals: A model for building a standardised hand-off protocol. *Journal on Quality and Patient Safety* 32(11): 646–55

Department of Health (2007) *Improvement leaders guide: General improvement skills.* Crown, London

Langley G, Nolan K, Nolan T, Norman C, Provost L (1996) *The improvement guide.* Jossey Bass, San Francisco

National Health Service Institute for Innovation and Improvement (NHSI) (2007) *The Improvement Leaders' Guide to Process Mapping, Analysis and Redesign. NHSIII* Available at: http://www.institute.nhs.uk/improvementleadersguide

Penny J (2003) In NHS Institute for Innovation and Improvement (2007) *The improvement leaders' guide - Delivering improvement: making it happen.* Available from: http//:www.institute.nhs.uk/improvementleadersguide

Further reading

Berwick DM (1996) A primer on leading the improvement of systems. *British Medical Journal* **312:** 619–22

National Health Service Institute for Innovation and Improvement (2010) *Creating the culture for innovation.* NHSI publications, Warwick University

National Health Service Institute for Innovation and Improvement (2010) *The handbook of quality and service improvement tools.* NHSI publications, Warwick University

Scholtes PR, Joiner BL, Streibel JL (2003) *The team handbook.* 3rd edn. Oriel Inc, Edison, NJ

Chapter 13

Theory into practice: a model to facilitate the integration of CPD

Introduction
Margaret McArthur and Rosemarie Mason

Lifelong learning is integral to clinical governance (Department of Health, 1998). It has been supported with a series of Government initiatives in recent years, which have emphasised a progressive commitment to the concept. Although not a new idea, greater accountability for clinical governance was recommended within *A first class service* (Department of Health, 1998) and it was further facilitated by the development of a framework for health and social care organisations to implement continuing professional development (CPD) in practice (Department of Health, 1999).

The NHS Plan (Department of Health, 2000) set out ways of co-ordinating the education of healthcare workers in order that quality of service would be enhanced by lifelong learning. This was supported by the development of *Working together – learning together* (Department of Health, 2001), which provided a framework for lifelong learning.

Clinical governance is also a necessary part of the Knowledge and Skills Framework introduced as part of the employment contract in Agenda for Change (Department of Health, 2004; 2005). In addition, since 2005 the continuation of registration with the Health Professions Council is dependent on registrants being able to demonstrate a commitment to continued learning. Every two years a proportion of registrants is required to submit a profile of their CPD activity for audit (Health Professions Council, 2006). Regulation and re-registration is now dependant on the demonstration of clearly documented and accountable continuous learning (Department of Health, 2006; 2007; 2009).

One of the aims of appropriately managed CPD programmes is to attract, motivate and retain high calibre healthcare staff, but attention needs to be paid to how can this be achieved within pressured organisational environments. This chapter discusses a particular model of CPD delivery that is a successful way of introducing viable CPD activity into the workplace.

171

The CPD challenges

Among allied health professions there is a wide variety of CPD activity in evidence (McArthur and Jepson, 2002; McArthur and Mason, 2004) but there are factors that influence successful engagement in the activity and implementation of learning. A model of CPD needs to embody the following elements.

The need for action

Clinicians' main perception of CPD can be that it is something delivered through courses. It is seen as a re-registration need and as such is a cause of worry. Experiences of pre-registration education, personal striving, and the needs of the job can set expectations of CPD. Successful realisations of those CPD expectations rely on good managerial support, peer support, departmental commitment, and a shared mission. The benefits of successful CPD activity include re-registration, enhanced motivation, thereby providing a focus for effort, evidence of ability, and improved professional confidence. This is offset by barriers to CPD, which include a work culture that does not support or value protected CPD activity, combined with work overload. This can engender feelings of guilt in those who endeavour to engage in CPD activities, and feelings of isolation as healthcare workers try individually to address their CPD needs, with a resulting lack of a shared mission.

Attrition of staff is the likely result of inadequate CPD activity (Sutton and Griffin 2000; Townsend 2006; Scanlon *et al* 2010). Particular factors that have an impact on CPD engagement include lack of encouragement, remote or ineffective management, and time pressure, with the fear that time spent on CPD is compromising client care.

Therefore, a collaborative assessment of need, producing an agreed understanding of service development needs results in shared ownership of both the potential challenges and the possible solutions. The collaboration between all levels of service delivery engenders a sense of shared responsibility for identifying the issues, devising the action plan and evaluating the success of that action plan.

The need to make it worth while

Most allied health professions expect that they should be actively engaged in CPD but personal striving and being self-directed are not sufficient to maintain motivation to persist with lifelong learning: there needs to be tangible evidence that doing it is worth while. Where CPD is given a high profile by the organisation it is perceived as a reflection of the positive value placed on the contribution of the profession to the service. Therefore, good managerial and peer support and the resulting collegiality are important so that a service shares a mission to improve its healthcare provision. This shared mission generates a willingness within individuals to strive for enhancement of their own skills by engendering a sense that people are supported in a collaborative effort to learn and develop.

Perceptible benefits

Along with benefits that could include increased motivation, evidence of clinical ability and increased confidence, a co-ordinated approach to CPD also has pragmatic results. The Knowledge and Skills Framework (KSF) is an outcome-based competency framework that has been introduced as a requirement for Agenda for Change (Department of Health 2004; 2005). All jobs within the NHS have been described within an outline of listed competencies under a number of dimensions (see *Figure 13.1*).

The core dimensions that are highlighted in the KSF and are judged within Agenda for Change are now being influenced by the NHS White Paper, *Equity and excellence: Liberating the NHS* (Department of Health, 2010). This redefines the principles of effective, focused, and responsive client-centred care, delivered by healthcare workers who are able, empowered and innovative in their service delivery. This is now being operationalised through the evolving NHS initiative Quality, Innovation, Prevention, Productivity (QUIPP) (Health Foundation, 2010) which has established a national programme of workstreams focusing on safe care, right care, long-term conditions, urgent care, and end of life care. Therefore, a work-based, service development-driven CPD programme, such as the one suggested here, will allow health and social care workers, who have many demands on their time and resources, to respond to these types of evolving initiatives that are aimed at improving quality and productivity across care pathways.

Within these governance processes health and social care workers are required to demonstrate their ability to meet these service delivery challenges by providing evidence of their fitness for the purpose of the job, in a process of professional development review. There is an expectation that CPD will be integral to this process. Where people can see the connection between CPD and their performance review and development appraisal process they are more likely

Figure 13.1. KSF competencies.

to be motivated to undertake it. Similarly, if the same CPD activity could be used in preparation for an HPC audit where the aim is to prove continued fitness to practise for the purpose of re-registration, then that would prevent unnecessary duplication of effort. Therefore, a CPD model needs to facilitate 'smart' thinking where a single activity can be used for multiple purposes (Morley, 2009).

The task needs to be manageable and achievable

Healthcare workers are time constrained and likely to consider that contact time with clients is their priority. They commonly struggle to cope with balancing the need to manage their workload with the need to demonstrate personal development (McArthur and Jepson, 2002; McArthur and Mason, 2004). CPD activity may not only be problematic to implement but also the associated documentation can be regarded as difficult and time-consuming. The wider benefits, to client care and of individuals improving their own performance, are lost in the daily battle to 'get things done'. CPD may be regarded as something 'additional' to the job specification, rather than being an integral part of it. Without appropriate support or in cases where management is remote or ineffective, CPD is likely to be given a low priority. CPD therefore needs to be easy to undertake and document and should be integrated into a daily routine.

Working in partnership

The Department of Health guidance (Department of Health 1999; 2001) stresses the importance of partnership between individuals and the organisations for which they work. The main emphasis is on working more collaboratively to promote consistency of standards via work-based and team learning. The intention is that the relationship should be one of mutual benefit where all stakeholders can thrive. Managers have a role in creating a work environment which encourages life-long learning whilst providing support to co-ordinate individual and organisational needs. People can be motivated to undertake CPD if there is a shared focus of effort and if it helps them to respond to service delivery challenges. When this is evident a greater sense of team and professional identity ensues. Partnership, in which there is collaboration between all levels of a service, where each individual can be involved at an appropriate level and individual preferences can be accommodated, are important aspects of CPD implementation. This flexible way of working also has the potential to provide people with a louder voice: a cohesive team being more likely to act in the interests of client advocacy.

The collaborations in CPD (CCPD) model: a solution

Individual CPD activity should be reconsidered. McArthur and Mason (2004) have identified that CPD as an individual endeavour can be haphazard, unfocused and requiring high levels of motivation. Without consistent peer or managerial support it can be rather isolating. Individuals trying to do their best within time constraints are less likely to consider that the cost of spending time on CPD and away from clients is worth any perceived benefit. In order to motivate healthcare workers to appreciate the value of CPD in personal and organisational terms it should be defined as a service/departmental issue. In reality it should:

• Be a strategic development rather than an individual endeavour
• Be a simple and agreed plan of action resulting in a team project rather than a lone voice against adversity

- Satisfy stakeholder(s) standards and so be informed by theory but be part of practice development.

The School of Allied Health Professions at the University of East Anglia has developed the collaborations in continuing professional development (CCPD) model (see *Figure 13.2*). In effect, it runs like an action research project in that there is a shared definition of the problem, a collaborative agreement on how the problem should be solved, coupled with a shared evaluation (Hart and Bond, 1995).

The six stages of the CCPD model

- **Identification of a problem** — the team will identify a range of service development issues
- **Discussion and negotiation** — discussions need to take place to identify the most current service development focus and which areas to address first; every member of the team potentially has a part to play in that discussion
- **Implementation** — plans are then made about how to address the identified service development issues and the role each team member will take
- **On-going evaluation** — an appropriate timeframe for initial evaluation is

Figure 13.2. The CCPD model.

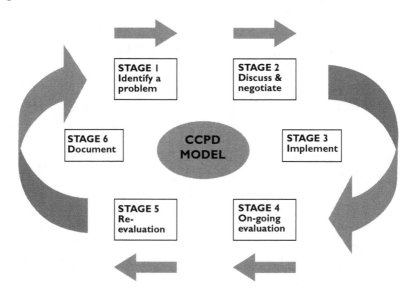

agreed, along with the most appropriate outcome measures, enabling fine tuning of the original project plan

- **Re-evaluation** – these outcome measures and individual feedback monitor the effectiveness of the plan. If the service development issue has been resolved the team can move on to the next issue; if not, there is an opportunity to engage in further cycles of problem identification, negotiation, implementation and evaluation.

- **Documentation** — There is shared responsibility for recording results. Each member of the team will have a responsibility for documenting their part in the service development. The result is a composite document that everyone contributes to. It provides evidence of CPD, service development and team working; there is a shared agenda and a solution to the problem.

These stages can be illustrated through two practice examples. In the first example (*Table 13.1*), occupational therapists were working on a definition of their contribution to the delivery of a particular service. The learning goal was developed after preliminary work was undertaken by the team on identifying the core OT role within this service.

The learning goal was agreed, following the first two stages of 'identifying the problem' and 'discussing and negotiating' the action plan. The strategies and resources were part of the 'implementation phase', while the evaluation focused on 'what was to be assessed'. The identified evidence fulfilled the 'documentation' element of the process.

The result was an enhanced understanding of the OT role which produced the template for what OTs were able to offer. This then informed the development of a service specification which would clarify the overall OT contribution within a skills review. The next step was to further identify additional issues, and the CCPD model cycle continued.

The identification of the problem, in the second example (*Table 13.2*), centred on being able to establish the effectiveness of a physiotherapy service. Following discussion and negotiation it was agreed that outcome measures were one way of demonstrating effectiveness. The strategies and resources in the example show how the plan was implemented. The outcome measures were appraised as part of the evaluation phase and matched against local, national and Government priorities. The summary of the capacity to demonstrate the contribution of physiotherapists to the service provided the documentation phase of the model.

The next step was to generate a protocol outlining the most appropriate outcome measures to be used and this plan will go through the same cyclical, CCPD process.

Table 13.1. Practice example 1			
Learning goals	**Strategies and resources**	**What is to be assessed?**	**Evidence**
Developing the service specification within the context of a health skills review	*Resources:* Electronic databases Policy documents University facilitator *Strategies:* Search electronic databases Review policy documents Explore occupational science literature (the theoretical underpinning for OT practice)	The OT role in the sevice The evidence base and policy context that will support the ongoing provision of services	A completed and adopted service specification for OTs in this service

Table 13.2. Practice example 2			
Learning goals	**Strategies and resources**	**What is to be assessed?**	**Evidence**
To identify standardised outcome measures in current use across the service	*Resources:* Review current common practice Existing department resources Case records Electronic databases *Strategies:* Find and copy all examples	The number of outcome measures and the range of what they assess The degree to which they harmonise with local, national and Government priorities	Copies of outcome measures Summary of review of utility and efficacy of the measures in use Summary of review of the capacity to demonstrate the contribution of physiotherapists to the service

Conclusion

Past experience of using the CCPD model has indicated that there are a number of benefits to this type of collaborative working.

Organisation

The CCPD model allows for setting a task that accommodates the needs of each level of service development and potentially each member of the team.

Efficiency

The CCPD model improves personal and service development and therefore facilitates people to fulfil CPD requirements by:

*   **Working smarter** — CPD activities are more focused and streamlined
*   **Enabling modernisation** — it improves service delivery because it is service needs led and it is matched to stakeholder agendas. In addition it is collaborative, a watchword of Government initiatives
*   **Enabling staff** — it has flexibility as it can be extended to a wide variety of team memberships so that each individual can be involved at the appropriate level and therefore individual preference can be accommodated
*   **Sharing ownership** — collaboration between all levels of the service ensures that there is there is equal responsibility for the ownership of the service development issue. The people leading the CCPD activities co-ordinate above and below; 'doing with' rather than being 'done to', ensuring that no one is a passive recipient of disembodied edicts from on high
*   **Promoting inherent worth** — it gives permission to engage in the activity. This offers employee recognition of the importance of CPD involvement thereby facilitating a supportive environment
*   **Embedding evidence-based practice** — CPD is embedded into practice and professional culture so that CPD is not seen as a separate entity. It can help to ensure that health workers are not only fit for practice but also fit for purpose
*   **Enhancing transferable skills** — this generic model could be used within any profession. This is particularly so because the agenda is set by the participants and the solutions arise from their own professional understanding of the situation.

This model therefore meets a wide range of personal, professional and service development requirements by being responsive to change and reflective of need. In addition, by being work-based and flexible it empowers people and encourages a culture of cohesive teamworking.

Key points

- Engagement in CPD is challenging for AHPs
- Successful CPD activity enhances job satisfaction and ensures continuing fitness to practice
- The CCPD model meets a wide range of personal, professional and service development needs and promotes effective and partnership working

Acknowledgements
We would like to express our thanks to the Workforce Development Group of the South West London Strategic Health Authority for commissioning the original research which informed the development of the model. Thanks also to occupational therapy colleagues who collaborated in the research.

References

Department of Health (1998) *A first class service.* Available from: www.dh.gov.uk

Department of Health (1999) *Continuing professional development. Quality in the new NHS.* Available from: www.dh.gov.uk

Department of Health (2000) *The NHS plan.* Available from: www.dh.gov.uk

Department of Health (2001) *Working together – learning together. A framework for life-long learning for the NHS.* Available from: www.dh.gov.uk

Department of Health (2004) *The NHS knowledge and skills framework.* Available from: www.dh.gov.uk

Department of Health (2005) *Agenda for change: Terms and conditions handbook.* Available from: www.dh.gov.uk

Department of Health (2006) *The regulation of the non-medical healthcare professions: A review by the Department of Health.* Available from: www.dh.gov.uk

Department of Health (2007) *Trust, assurance and safety – The regulation of health pro-*

fessionals in the 21st century. Available from: www.dh.gov.uk

Department of Health (2009) *NHS 2010–2015: From good to great. Preventative, people-centred, productive.* Available from: www.dh.gov.uk

Department of Health (2010) *Equity and excellence: Liberating the NHS.* London DoH Available from: http://www.dh.gov.uk/dr_consum_dh/groups/dh_digitalassets/@ dh/@en/@ps/documents/digitalasset/dh_117794.pdf [Accessed 3 March 2011]

Hart E, Bond M (1995) *Action research for health and social care.* Open University Press, Buckingham

Health Foundation (2010) *Quest for quality and improved performance.* Available from: http://www.health.org.uk/areas-of-work/research/quest-for-quality-and-improved-performance/ [Accessed 15 April 2011]

Health Professions Council (2006) *Continuing professional development and your registration.* Available from: http://www.hpc-uk.org/assets/documents/10001314CPD_and_your_registration.pdf

McArthur M, Jepson J (2002) *Innovation for career development. A report on the current continuing professional development needs for allied health professionals.* School of Occupational Therapy and Physiotherapy, University of East Anglia

McArthur M, Mason R (2004) *Theory into practice – A model to facilitate the integration of CPD for health and social care professionals.* School of Allied Health Professions, University of East Anglia

Morley M (2009) *Preceptorship handbook for occupational therapists.* 2nd edn. College of Occupational Therapists, London

Scanlan JN, Still M, Stewart K, Croaker J (2010) Recruitment and retention issues for occupational therapists in mental health: Balancing the pull and the push. *Australian Occupational Therapy Journal* **57**(2): 102–10

Sutton G, Griffin MA (2000) Transition from student to practitioner: The role of expectations, values and personality. *British Journal of Occupational Therapy* **63**(8): 380–8

Townsend E (2006) Effects of workplace policy on continuing professional development: The case of occupational therapy in Nova Scotia, Canada. *Canadian Journal of Occupational Therapy* **73**(2): 98–108

The evolution of a continuing education programme for AHPs: an action research approach

Introduction

Adrian MM Schoo, Karen E Stagnitti and Kevin P McNamara

Allied health professionals increasingly need continuing education (CE) that complies with requirements for registration and re-accreditation. CE involves lifelong learning to improve and maintain competencies and standards of care (Hunter and Nicol, 2002; Shillitoe *et al*, 2002). Younger allied health professionals (AHPs) and those further removed from regional centres find poor access to CE a major barrier in rural employment (Belcher *et al*, 2005). Additional benefits of CE reported in the allied health literature include enhanced workforce retention (Smith *et al*, 1995; Hunter and Nicol, 2002; Belcher *et al*, 2005), peer motivation (Driesen *et al*, 2005), feelings of personal accomplishment, reduced risk of professional burnout (Schlenz *et al*, 1995), and job satisfaction (Solomon *et al*, 2001).

Research from south-west Victoria, Australia, showed that AHPs wished to access CE more than four times per year (Stagnitti *et al*, 2005). In addition to formal in-service CE there was a need for specific CE on request which was preferably hands-on (Stagnitti *et al*, 2005). The major challenge for CE programmes is to allow interaction between attendees and presenters, and to develop programmes that are accessible and perceived as meaningful to geographically dispersed health professionals. This is especially important in rural areas where the viability of CE programmes requires a strong attendance from a smaller cohort of practitioners. Given the positive effect of interactivity on clinical practice (Thomson O'Brien *et al*, 2006) and increased access to video conference facilities (McNamara, 2006), providing CE with interactive learning to geographically dispersed health professionals may no longer be insurmountable.

Action research framework

Action research is a method of research that informs practice and brings together practitioners and researchers acting together on a cycle of activity (Avison *et al*, 1999). It can be used to monitor organisational process and the change-related dynamics required to effectively implement programmes (Avison *et al*, 1999). Action research is a cyclical process which begins with a determination of the initial problem, then continues in a spiral of planning, action (implementation), monitoring progress, evaluation, and reflection. Street (2003) suggests six criteria that can be used to determine whether action research is achieved. These criteria state that the research should be:

• Issue and outcome-based
• Cyclical
• Knowledge in action
• Participatory and democratic
• Educative, developmental and responsive
• Credible, sustainable and transferable.

Following the findings of Stagnitti *et al* (2005), the problem of easy access to CE for rural AHPs was identified in the geographical area of south-west Victoria, Australia. The region is classified as accessible/moderately accessible on the Accessibility/Remoteness Index of Australia (Hugo, 2002). This chapter describes the development, implementation, evaluation and reflections on a CE programme in this region delivered by the Greater Green Triangle University Department of Rural Health. The programme is co-ordinated from Hamilton which is centrally located in the region, approximately 1–2 hours drive from the peripheral parts of the region and 3.5 hours from Melbourne, Victoria's State capital. The Victorian Department of Human Services provided a grant to the Greater Green Triangle University Department of Rural Health (formed as a result of a partnership between Flinders and Deakin Universities) to develop and implement an allied health workforce recruitment and retention project, starting with physiotherapy. The CE programme was part of this. The first author led the project, building on earlier work of the second author. The third author led a CE programme for rural pharmacists. No such programme had previously been run in the region. Continuous evaluation of the programme was measured by attendance levels throughout the CE programme and satisfaction with the education received in terms of perceived clinical benefits.

Programme development

Once the problem of lack of easy access to continuing education for AHPs was identified, a needs assessment consisting of two surveys was sent to all physiotherapists in the region. The surveys aimed to establish appropriate content and format for education delivery. In this way, the surveys enabled all physiotherapists in the region to provide input into what would be their CE programme.

In March 2004 a small survey was sent to the two regional physiotherapy groups of the Australian Physiotherapy Association (APA) in south-west Victoria to be distributed among its members. Physiotherapy was targeted as the first profession to begin the programme because approximately 70–75 physiotherapists worked in the region – the majority full-time (58.1%) – with minimal locally available CE.

The first survey obtained a snapshot of CE needs, and established whether the results were in line with those reported in the literature, as well as the 2003 internal survey by one of the regional groups. Based on earlier surveys by Services for Australian Rural and Remote Allied Health (SARRAH) (2000) and O'Reilly (2002), the first survey determined suitable times and frequencies for CE activities in addition to preferred education topics for local delivery. Eleven of the 25 surveys were returned. A total of 72.7% of respondents favoured conducting professional development activities in the evening with 45.5% favouring early evenings; 36% preferred bimonthly attendance. Most respondents nominated topics of clinical relevance. The results of the surveys justified development of workshops and presentation sessions on topics of interest that could be delivered locally (e.g. in a local clinic) as requested.

These findings are in line with existing rural allied health reports (SARRAH, 2000; O'Reilly, 2002) and a 2003 survey in South West Barwon (Stagnitti *et al*, 2005). Late afternoons and early evenings have been found to be suitable for rural Victorian professionals of both the public and private sectors (O'Reilly, 2002). Reports have shown a need for clinical training on demand, opportunities to network, and and a need to develop skills such as evidence-based research and intervention (SARRAH, 2000; O'Reilly, 2002; Stagnitti *et al*, 2005). With support from the physiotherapists in the region, the agreed format of the evening workshops and presentations was 6:00 pm for a 6:30 pm start (with refreshments), a short break for interaction with the presenter or with peers, contents that could be practised or that had clear practical applicability, and time for questions at the end.

In August 2004 a second survey was distributed to 70 physiotherapists (including non-members of the APA) in the region, with the aim of clarifying and confirming the areas that physiotherapists wanted to cover in their CE programme. This survey, adapted with permission from the Queensland branch of the APA, asked physiotherapists to indicate all course topics of interest. Thirty-one of the 70 questionnaires were returned (44.3%). Although the results of the survey showed that most physiotherapists had a musculoskeletal CE interest and preferred musculoskeletal topics rather than neurological or cardiothoracic topics, some practical considerations favoured alternating musculoskeletal topics with topics in other areas.

Substantial ownership of the developmental process was then given to all physiotherapists, regardless of position or place of work. The aim of giving ownership of the process to the participants of the CE programme was to enhance ease of attendance and to promote the perception of clinical applicability and relevance arising from continuing education among rural physiotherapists.

Implementation

Based on the first survey, which also tapped into immediate CE needs, the programme commenced at the start of July 2004. Once CE needs had been explored the programme was further developed and a calendar of events was distributed to the physiotherapists. The programme was based on physiotherapists' requests, and included evidence-based presentations and a minimum of 25% of the session time was assigned to practice skills and for interaction. Sessions were held once a month; some were given as presentations (with a mix of approximately 75% theory and 25% practice) and others were held as workshops (where the majority of time was spent practising). In addition, there were clinical topics that could be delivered 'on site' and that offered participants substantial time to practice (more than 75% of the session time).

The education delivered during the programme was deliberately designed to be relevant and clinically applicable, in keeping with the principles of adult learning. Presenters were instructed that a minimum of a quarter of the content should focus on practical application. Written participant feedback, using an evaluation form, was sought after each session or workshop as a means of continuous quality improvement of the format.

Evaluation

In advance of this programme being made available to other professions and before video-conferencing was made an option, the following targets were set:

- Attendance at a minimum of four CE sessions by 50% of survey respondents
- Ratings of usefulness for clinical practice equalling or exceeding five on a seven-point Likert scale of perception of clinical applicability, with seven being highly applicable.

Attendance

To ascertain if the programme met the first target, attendance at CE sessions for physiotherapists held between the start of July 2004 and the end of August 2005 were measured (*Table 14.1*). More than half (57.2%) of the physiotherapists in the region attended a minimum of four sessions and 68.6% attended at least one 'on-site' workshop. Only 17.1% of the physiotherapists did not attend at all. Numbers attending sessions were consistently high (about 25–40% of physiotherapists in the region). In addition, 22.9% attended at least one course (i.e. clinical pilates or myofascial dry needling) and 68.6% attended at least one workshop 'in clinic' delivered at the participants' workplace. More than two-thirds of the physiotherapists (68.6%) knew of others who attended at least one of the CE functions of the 2004/5 programme and 45.7% of these physiotherapists received useful information from others who attended. Four CE sessions a year was the number of educational activities found to be preferred by health workers in a survey of AHPs in same area of the CE programme (Stagnitti *et al*, 2005).

Table 14.1. Frequency of physiotherapy attendance at the 2004/2005 CE programme (*n* = 35)	
Attended	**%**
None of the sessions	17.1%
One of the sessions	14.3%
Two of the sessions	11.4%
Three of the sessions	0%
Four or more sessions	57.2%

Usefulness for clinical practice

To ascertain if the programme met the second target, ratings of usefulness for clinical practice were gathered from participant evaluation forms. More than 60% of participants completed the evaluation form at the end of individual CE functions. *Table 14.2* presents the cumulative data on the evaluation of usefulness of workshops, based on a just over 60% response rate from 365 attendees to the CE programme. As physiotherapists attended multiple sessions, and evaluation forms were anonymous to increase the likelihood of honest feedback, each attendee to each session was counted. This resulted in 221 evaluation form responses. The evaluation showed that the median and mode of the Likert scale of perceived clinical usefulness of the programme exceeded five. In fact the programme was perceived by attendees to warrant a maximum score of seven. Although self-reported application of educational activities into clinical practice is unreliable (Dunning *et al*, 2004), it is commonly used in the literature when other measures are not justified. Since the CE programme included a range of topics and allowed selective attendance, testing knowledge or application of the entire programme was inappropriate.

Effect on clinical skills

A third survey (*Figure 14.1*) was mailed out in August 2005 to the 75 regional physiotherapists who had participated in the CE programme. The survey received

Table 14.2. Perceived usefulness of CE workshops and presentations measured by seven-point Likert scale*

Item	Mode	Median
Suitability of the venue	7	7
Presenter style	7	7
Content	7	7
Applicability to clinical practice	7	7
Overall impression	7	7

*Minimum score =1, Maximum score = 7. Percentage of participants who completed the evaluation form at the time of the workshop was 60.5% (*n* = 221)

Professional development and clinical practice survey

Have you attended any of the physiotherapy clinical workshops or presentations (in person or by videoconference network) conducted by the Greater Green Triangle University Department of Rural Health (Greater Health) in the Education Centre of the Hamilton Hospital (e.g. clinical Pilates, taping, soft tissue injury management)?
• I have attended 0 / 1 / 2 / 3 / more than 3 workshops or presentations

Have you attended any of the physiotherapy clinical workshops or presentations conducted by Greater Health in your local area (e.g., sacroiliac joint assessment and treatment, use of valid and reliable outcome measures)?
• Yes / No

Have you attended any of the clinical courses facilitated by Greater Health (e.g. myofascial dry needling, clinical Pilates)?
• None / dry needling / clinical Pilates

Do you know of others who have attended any of the above workshops, presentations or courses?
• Yes / No

Have you received useful information from others who have attended any of the above clinical workshops, presentations or courses?
• Yes / No

What has been the direct or indirect effect of any of the above workshops, presentations or courses on your clinical skills and the way you work?
• It has made no / some / a large difference in my clinical skills
• It has made no / some / a large difference in the way I assess patients
• It has made no / some / a large difference in the way I treat patients
• It has made no / some / a large difference in the number of patients who visit me for clinical reasons

Other comments:

Figure 14.1. Professional development and clinical practice survey.

ethical approval from the Flinders University Social and Behavioural Research Ethics Committee. This survey explored the perceived effect of the 2004/2005 CE programme on clinical physiotherapy skills.

Before distribution, the six questions on the survey were examined by a panel of four experts and were found to have face validity. Four questions were related to attendance and two questions asked about the quality of information and perceived effect on clinical skills. All participants provided informed consent. Data were analysed using Excel and SPSS statistical software. Appropriate descriptive statistics were calculated based on the nature of the dataset and its distribution. A return rate of 46.7% ($n = 35$) was gained for the third survey. The results of the third survey showed that the interactive CE programme had a positive influence on perceived clinical skills (*Table 14.3*).

Overall

Satisfaction with the CE programme was extremely high, with organisation of the sessions and perceived clinical relevance rated highly. Qualitative comments supported the relevance of the programme items to clinical practice, the calibre of the presenters and the positive effects on clinical skills and patient outcomes. The frequency of attendance, whether in person or via video-conferencing, was high.

Table 14.3. Perceived effect of the 2004/2005 programme on clinical skills and the number of patients visiting the clinic ($n = 35$)			
	Percentage of respondents		
Outcome	**No effect†**	**Some effect**	**Large effect**
On clinical skills	11.4%	68.6%	20.0%
On patient assessment	20.0%	60.0%	20.0%
On patient treatment	17.1%	60.0%	22.9%
On the number of patients	68.6%	20.6%	8.8%
† Two of the respondents noted 'no perceived effect'. Although they did not practise at the time they have been included in the results			

Reflection on the programme

Needs assessment

The first two surveys were used to establish the professional needs of physiotherapists in the region and to develop and implement the CE programme. This is an accepted method for identifying professional CE needs (Owen, 2006). It was used to inform content as well as context of the programme so that the physiotherapists in the region could take ownership of the CPD programme and their participation. There is evidence to suggest that perception-based needs assessment, i.e. asking participants what they need, is a subjective process which has the potential to produce different results to other types of structured needs assessments (Cervero, 2001). Therefore, this process could more accurately be seen as a means of identifying the education that local participants would value. Therefore perhaps, a perceived improvement in clinical performance should be considered in terms of the effect it has in encouraging attendance at CE programmes rather than an actual measure of improved performance.

Programme content

The content of the CE programme was predominantly on practice and clinical reasoning. There is evidence from medical research that self-directed CE might encourage participants to stay within their 'comfort zone' (Sibley *et al*, 1982). This influenced the decision not to focus exclusively on musculoskeletal topics despite participant preferences. In addition, the format of the monthly workshops and on-site training sessions of the CE programme were based on principles of adult learning to optimise the potential effect of the programme on clinical skills (Spencer and Jordan, 1999).

Efficacy

The continuous evaluation of the programme provided some evidence that transfer of knowledge and skills had taken place. Most physiotherapists reported improved perceived clinical skills and some physiotherapists reported perceived increased patient demand. The evaluation did not allow the separation of the combined effect of needs-based demand, programme content, the interactive delivery or the initial excitement of having access to rural CE. Kirkpatrick (1994) described four levels of CE effect evaluation and Gusky (2000) suggests five levels. This study provides evidence of learning (level two) and potential implementation of learning among the rural participants. Direct evidence of improved clinical practice and patient outcomes was outside the scope of this project, although some qualitative comments made reference to this level. For example, the newly acquired knowledge and skills led to frequent positive comments on implications for clinical practice.

Personal conversation with one of the physiotherapy registration boards also confirmed that the current CE programme assists with the re-registration of physiotherapists who have let their registration lapse (Personal communication, August 2006). This is likely to be similar for other professions that have mandatory registration and CE requirements. As such, needs-based rural CE programmes can be a valuable tool to build rural workforce capacity, although the influence of these programmes on recruitment and retention remains to be tested by controlled studies.

Implementation and delivery

The practitioner-centred approach to programming may have aided the high levels of satisfaction with the education provided. The factors that are often reported to negate CE programmes, such as access issues, costs, poor applicability to clinical practice and lack of practical content in CE activities were successfully addressed in the 2004/5 programme. It is evident that the respondents to the third survey did not feel these negative constraints. Participants valued locally presented workshops with presenters who were highly qualified. Where travel was involved, participants valued its recognition, with the supply of food and drinks, for example.

Access to CE can be improved by technologies such as tele/video/virtual conferencing, electronic mail, videotapes and print materials (Hughes, 1998; Sheppard and Mackintosh, 1998). Video-conferencing was offered during the programme.

Findings of a systematic review of 32 studies (30 randomised control studies) demonstrated that lectures alone (i.e. passive dissemination of information) were not sufficient to change clinical practice, but that interactive workshops had a moderately large effect (Thomson O'Brien *et al*, 2006). The Australian

Physiotherapy Association (1998) demands that members undertake approximately 30 hours of formal and informal learning a year. It is suggested by the authors that a formal planning process allowed the delivery of a tailored CE structure that was valued by participants and matched their needs in terms of desired content, delivery and number of CE hours that were available. A deliberately interactive approach to teaching may have enhanced appreciation of the course content. This model has the potential to be used more widely in the development of CE for physiotherapists.

Other health professionals

The continuing education programme was initially developed in response to identified regional clinical physiotherapists' needs, which cannot be generalised to all professions. For example, Dunbar and Franklin (2004) found nursing staff preferred having education timed for their working hours (mid-afternoon, while shifts overlap).

In view of our programme's success in meeting the targets of attendance and usefulness for clinical practice, we considered its application to other AHPs. Professionals from other disciplines had begun asking whether they too could access the programme. Qualitative comments also reinforced the notion that the programme format was relevant to clinical practice in a rural setting and to other professional groups such as occupational therapists, podiatrists, prosthetists and orthotists.

The 2005/6 CE programme was therefore expanded to include other AHPs and greater access was created by video-conferencing. There was no evidence to suggest that access via video-conference had a detrimental effect on the quality and outcome of the interactive workshops. Acceptability of video-conferencing was measured by a separate survey of those who used this medium during the period between August 2005 and August 2006 ($n = 15$). The survey form was an adaptation of that used to investigate the views of pharmacists in the same region (McNamara, 2006). Reported problems related to sound, overheads, and learning practical clinical skills. Broadcasts at a minimum frequency of 384kbps were best received. Video-conferencing was perceived as an acceptable method to increase attendance at CE, and some of those who used it indicated their intention to increase their use of this medium. Although findings are consistent with those of a CE programme for rural pharmacists (McNamara, 2006), this area requires further investigation.

Development into a state-wide programme

In 2007 the programme developed into a state-wide Victorian CE programme for 22 allied health groups. The programme was also expanded to be accessible in person, via video-conference, live streaming or retrospective viewing via the internet. Although retrospective viewing does not give professionals the opportunity to interact, it allows them to access CE at a time that suits them. This programme has an extensive evaluation framework, which includes sessional evaluation based on learning objectives, and skills and competencies learnt, as well as pre-programme and follow-up surveys. Access to the programme remains free and the content of sessions is of interest to more than one discipline. In line with findings of an earlier survey on managerial issues (Stagnitti *et al*, 2006) the programme includes a two-day personal effectiveness training course which aims to improve self-management, team skills and leadership. From 2008, the programme was further expanded and recorded sessions of the CE programme can be accessed by professionals in other states in Australia via the internet. Also, non-clinical content was added to affirm professionals' experiences in their roles (see update at the end of this chapter).

Strengths and limitations

Using the six criteria of action research (Street, 2003) the following strengths and limitations of this project need to be considered:

• There is an undisputed shortage of education opportunities for rural health professionals, and it is reasonable to suggest that issues of practical, context-specific knowledge are addressed through this CE programme
• Three cycles have been included in this chapter. Ongoing open cycles enable the programme to develop further in relation to its content and expansion in Australia and across professions. This requires ongoing monitoring, analysis, evaluation, reflection, and modification
• Knowledge is tested in action and in context. Outcomes from CE programme evaluations have and continue to be used to modify further action and correspondingly, modifications are subsequently evaluated to test the theory developed from the previous evaluation
• Action research requires involvement of all participants who will be affected by the new knowledge or changes. Although only those who responded to the

surveys could be included in the analyses, all participants were involved in the process from the start through the needs assessment and informal input. Although it is a leap to infer ownership, participation in the development process was encouraged through repeated formal feedback mechanisms, and the high attendance rates suggest that participants supported the process

- Change through acquiring knowledge and learning new strategies needs to be sustainable. Although the second cycle showed that participants learnt and informed others, this aspect could have been explored in greater detail. The large proportion of local physiotherapists participating does, however, support the notion that this CE programme has sufficient impact on its own to influence local professional attitudes and capacity

- In relation to improvements over time, the programme first became a state-wide programme and then expanded into other states in Australia. The evaluation framework is much more extensive to assist the monitoring of programme expansion, and to analyse, evaluate, reflect and further modify the programme. This is crucial as more professionals and professions access the programme. The concept of this action research based programme is transferable to other professional groups and to other countries. Interstate expansion also facilitates the sustainability of the programme through a broader base of funding sources, and through increasing input from stakeholders with a wide variety of skills and experience.

Conclusion

This action research project was set up to address the CE needs of rural physiotherapists, who are known to face barriers in accessing the education required to maintain and improve competencies and standards of care (Belcher *et al*, 2005).

Evaluation of the CE programme delivered in 2004/5, which integrated the use of needs-based education, adult learning principles and an interactive workshop format, suggest that the programme was acceptable to attendees and benefited rural physiotherapists. The programme was well-attended and, following its initial implementation, access was requested from other professions. In response to this, the 2005/6 programme was extended to other AHPs, with enhanced access from video-conference broadcasts. In 2007, the CE programme evolved into a state-wide programme with an extensive evaluation framework. Since then it has expanded interstate.

This CE project illustrates that action research can be used successfully to develop and implement a national needs-based programme, both within and across the allied health professions, that seeks and implements continuous improvement.

Acknowledgements
This study was supported by grants from the Victorian Department of Human Services and was originally published in the International Journal of Therapy and Rehabilitation in 2008.

An update: non-clinical content of the CE programme

Affirming the experience of AHPs through continuing education

The programme now also includes non-clinical content and this section is an update on the non-clinical evolution of the now national programme.

Changing models of care necessitate more than clinical skills to include enhanced inter-professional practice and teamwork with possible role redesign and managing increasing workloads. Effective functioning in a changing work environment also requires organisational skills (Lincoln *et al*, 2001) that are generally not developed during undergraduate training. These include leadership, management, communication and interpersonal skills (Lin *et al*, 2009). Suboptimal management in allied health has been associated with compromised intention to stay in rural positions (Stagnitti *et al*, 2006) and it seems obvious that organisational skills are increasingly important to function well in contemporary team-based care. Interestingly, the focus of the leadership literature is moving from the individual to collective leadership and teamwork.

Training in organisational skills such as time management, negotiation and conflict resolution is likely to assist AHPs in coping better with demanding work in public health settings that tend to be hierarchical (O'Toole *et al.*, 2008, Hernan *et al.*, 2009, National Health Service Scotland, 2009). As part of the action research project described earlier, and as a following iteration, the content of a non-clinical training programme was established by surveying the AHPs who accessed the state-wide CE programme 'CPDWorks' (Schoo *et al.*, 2009). As part of the survey, AHPs were invited to select work-related values, competencies and behaviours (Victorian Government Department of Human Services, 2005; Center for the Health Professions, 2006) that they perceived as important in everyday rural practice.

Pre-programme survey

The pre-programme survey was completed by 165 AHPs (47.8%). Most were female (85.5%). Mean age was 37 years. Physiotherapists (37.2%) and occupational therapists (15.1%) represented the majority of respondents. Factor analysis identified the values, competencies and behaviours that AHPs deemed most relevant for their work. Three robust variables could be constructed for: practice ethics, applied practice, and personal effectiveness (i.e. making good decisions, knowledge and improving management, problem solving, planning–implementation–evaluation, and building positive work environments). There was a significant difference between AHPs older than 30 years of age and those up to 30, with older AHPs recognising the importance of personal effectiveness. This was thought to be in line with natural career progression and requests for this type of training from older professionals.

Training to enhance personal effectiveness and teamwork

As with other CE sessions, the developed course was presented in accordance with the principles of adult education and was structured to address effectiveness (that is, personal effectiveness, group and interpersonal effectiveness, and organisational effectiveness). The aims of this non-clinical training were to: (1) enhance understanding of organisational context and process of healthcare; (2) facilitate development of individual empowerment and ownership of work; (3) give participants appropriate skills and tools to improve accomplishment; and (4) present them with tools for ongoing self-evaluation and development. This sides with the concept of learning organisations (Senge, 1994) and programmes elsewhere (Judkins *et al.*, 2006).

The training was initially delivered in a two-day format only (from early 2007 to the end of 2008). A one-day version was added later. Professionals who attended the one-day version were required to complete reading and questionnaires prior to the course.

Evaluation of the training

At the end of the training, 95% (n = 120) of course participants completed the evaluation. Results showed strong agreement (ranging from 86.2 to 93.5% agreement per objective) that this non-clinical training programme met its objectives.

197

The course included 12 topics: communication, understanding personality and listening styles, leadership styles, self-awareness, the power of vision, circles of influence and concern, choice theory, team and group effectiveness, time management, running effective meetings, managing conflict, and self-management. Participants rated conflict management (22.6%, $n = 38$), understanding personality styles (16.6%, $n = 28$), and team and group effectiveness (13.7%, $n = 23$) as most useful and relevant.

After 4–6 weeks participants were asked to complete a follow-up survey. The response rate was 42% ($n = 53$), with 41.5% ($n = 22$) having more than 10 years experience and 37.7% ($n = 20$) working as a group or team leader. Physiotherapists represented the largest group (24.5%, $n = 13$).

Participants reported greater awareness of their personal styles (e.g. communication and listening) and the impact of these on their work (79.2%, $n = 42$), and better awareness of group dynamics and their effect on performance (75.5%, $n = 40$). They commented on being more empowered to take ownership of their own self and professional development (71.7%, $n = 38$). Participants were also asked to rate the extent to which they experienced improvement, as compared to before the course, in relation to a number of statements linked to course objectives. The greatest improvement was noted in self-consciousness of how beliefs and perceptions influence behaviour, and greater proactivity and awareness of choices in how to respond to people or situations. Least improvement was noted in self-managing health and stress, and being effective in groups, with 50–60% reporting total improvement and the rest reporting extensive improvement or somewhat improved. Additional comments of 16 respondents indicated that the training improved self-awareness, time management and goal development. Other comments made by 21 participants included improved awareness of others, communication skills and leadership.

Discussion

Although workload can make it hard for professionals to attend the training, a single day is not sufficient to cover and absorb all relevant material and to practise new skills. To accommodate this, parts of the training content have been recorded and made available online so that participants can prepare. This then allows participants to attend one day instead of two, and where time for interaction during the training day is maximised.

Results of the follow-up survey are indicative that a number of participants reported positive outcomes four to six weeks after participating in this short training programme. At the same time, it is recognised that behaviour is difficult to change and that individualised feedback on performance could be embedded in the day-to-day working environment to reduce the chance that professionals revert back to their old behaviours. This could be achieved by peer coaching (Ackland, 1991). Peer coaching has been found to be effective for the purpose of disseminating knowledge, skills and experience to bring about change (Ladyshewsky, 2004) and could provide participants with the opportunity to support each other, learn from each other, practise new skills and develop metacognition.

Lastly, it is recognised that this study relied exclusively on self-assessment. A 360-degree feedback process could provide more objective data to record changes over time. This process requires a number of peers, subordinates and the line manager to rate the participant on a number of desirable values, competencies and behaviours.

In conclusion, the addition of non-clinical content into the CE programme was a positive step for allied health professionals.

Key points

- Rural physiotherapists are known to face barriers in accessing the education required to maintain and improve competencies and standards of care
- An interactive CE programme based on professional needs and adult learning principles was set up for rural physiotherapists in one region of south-west Victoria, Australia
- The programme was well-received and well-attended
- Perceived clinical usefulness of the interactive and CE programme was high and attendees perceived a positive influence of the programme on their clinical skills
- Accessing CE by video-conferencing can work well
- Programme contents can be of interest to more than one discipline, although preferred access time may differ for some of the disciplines
- The non-clinical content in CE courses for AHPs was reported to increase personal effectiveness

References

Ackland R (1991) A review of the peer coaching literature. *Journal of Staff Development* **12:** 22–7

Australian Physiotherapy Association (1998) *Professional development portfolio.* APA, Melbourne

Avison D, Lau F, Myers M, Nielsen PA (1999) Action research. *Communications of the ACM* **42**(1): 94–7

Belcher S, Kealey J, Jones J, Humphreys J (2005) *The VURHC Rural Allied Health Professionals Recruitment and Retention Study.* VURHC, Melbourne

Center for the Health Professions (2006) *Advanced leadership skills to build a safer health system.* San Francisco: University of California. Available from: http://www.futurehealth. ucsf.edu/Leadership/Portals/2/1006%20UCSF%20Case%20Study.pdf [Accessed 22 October 2008]

Cervero RM (2001) Continuing professional education in transition, 1981–2000. *International Journal of Lifelong Education* **20**(1/2): 16–30

Driesen A, Leemanns L, Baert H, Laekeman G (2005) Flemish community pharmacists' motivation and views related to continuing education. *Pharmacy World and Science* **27**(6): 447–52

Dunbar J, Franklin L (2004) *The Rural Intercampus Learning Environment Project: Integrating intranet technology into continuing education in the Barwon-South West Region. Project Evaluation Report.* Warrnambool, Greater Green Triangle University Department of Rural Health and SWARH

Dunning D, Heath C, Suls JM (2004) Flawed self-assessment. *Psychological Science in the Public Interest* **5**(3): 69–106

Gusky TR (2000) *Evaluating professional development.* Sage Publications, Thousand Oaks, CA

Hernan A, Schoo A, O'Toole K (2009) *Leaving the Bush: Why did they do it?* National Rural Health Conference. Cairns, Australia

Hughes R (1998) An omnibus survey of the Australian rural health dietetic workforce. *Australian Journal of Nutrition and Dietetics* **55**(4): 163–9

Hugo G (2002) Australia's changing non-metropolitan population. In: Wilkinson D, Blue I eds. *The new rural health.* Oxford University Press, Melbourne

Hunter E, Nicol M (2002) Systematic review: Evidence of the value of continuing professional development to enhance recruitment and retention of occupational therapists in mental health. *British Journal of Occupational Therapy* **65**(5): 207–15

Judkins S, Reid B, Furlow L (2006) Hardiness training among nurse managers: Building a healthy workplace. *Journal of Continuing Education in Nursing* **37**(5): 202–7

Kirkpatrick DL (1994) *Evaluating training programmes: The four levels.* Berett-Koehler, San

Francisco, CA

Ladyshewsky RK (2004) *What is peer coaching? When does it get results? Why does it work so well?* Available from: http://www.ceo-mentor.com.au/ceo-mentor/default. asp?newsID=1015024 [Accessed 9 December 2008]

Lin I, Beattie N, Spitz S, Ellis A, Spitz I (2009) Developing competencies for remote and rural senior allied health professionals in Western Australia. *Rural and Remote Health* **9**(2): 1115

Lincoln MA, Adamson BJ, Cant RV (2001) The importance of managerial competencies for new graduates in speech pathology. *Advances in Speech-Language Pathology* **3**(1): 25–36

McNamara KP (2006) Acceptability of videoconference technology for the delivery of continuing education to rural pharmacists. *Journal of Pharmacy Practice and Research* **36**(3): 187–9

National Health Service Scotland (2009) *Delivery through leadership: NHS Scotland Leadership Development Framework.* Available from: http://www.scotland.gov.uk/ Publications/2005/06/28112744/27466 [Accessed 21 May 2009]

O'Reilly C (2002) *Strengthening allied health in rural Victoria. A strategic programme to enhance professional education and capacity building.* Melbourne, Victorian Health Association & Allied Health Professions Alliance Victoria

O'Toole K, Schoo A, Stagnitti K, Cuss K (2008) Rethinking policies for rural allied health workforce retention: A social relations approach. *Health Policy* **87**(3): 326–32

Owen JM (2006) *Programme evaluation: Forms and approaches.* Allen & Unwin, Sydney

SARRAH (2000) *A study of allied health professionals in rural and remote Australia.* Services for Australian Rural & Remote Allied Health

Schlenz KC, Guthrie MR, Dudgeon B (1995) Burnout in occupational therapists and physical therapists working in head injury rehabilitation. *American Journal of Occupational Therapy* **49**(10): 986–93

Schoo AMM, O'Toole K, Hernan A, Gerber T (2009) *Improving personal, group and organisational effectiveness of allied health professionals who work in the public health sector.* Proceedings of the Loddon Mallee Allied Health Conference, 27 February Bendigo. Allied Health Network (Loddon Mallee Region)

Senge P (1994) *The fifth discipline: The art and practice of the learning organisation.* Currency Doubleday, New York

Sheppard L, Mackintosh S (1998) Technology in education: What is appropriate for rural and remote health professionals. *Australian Journal of Rural Health* **6**(4): 189–93

Shillitoe R, Eltringhan S, Green D (2002) Clinician, update thyself: Assessing the value of local training courses. *British Journal of Therapy and Rehabilitation* **9**(5): 166–70

Sibley JC, Sackett DL, Neufeld V, Gerrard B, Rudnick KV, Fraser W (1982) A randomized trial of continuing medical education. *New England Journal of Medicine* **306**(9): 511–5

Smith P, Schiller MR, Grant HK, Sachs L (1995) Recruitment and retention strategies used by occupational therapy directors in acute care, rehabilitation, and long-term-care settings. *American Journal of Occupational Therapy* **49**(5): 412–9

Solomon P, Salvatori P, Berry S (2001) Perceptions of important retention and recruitment factors by therapists in northwestern Ontario. *Journal of Rural Health* **17**(3): 278–85

Spencer JA, Jordan RK (1999) Learner centred approaches in medical education. *British Medical Journal* **318**(7193): 1280–3

Stagnitti K, Schoo A, Reid C, Dunbar J (2005) Access and attitude of rural allied health professionals to CPD and training. *International Journal of Therapy and Rehabilitation* **12**(8): 355–61

Stagnitti K, Schoo A, Reid C, Dunbar J (2006) An exploration of issues of management and intention to stay: Allied health professionals in South West Victoria. *Journal of Allied Health* **35**(4): 226–32

Street AF (2003) Action research. In: Minichello V, Sullivan G, Greenwood K, Axford R eds. *Handbook for research methods in nursing and health sciences.* 2nd edn. Pearson Education, Australia

Thomson O'Brien MA, Freemantle N, Oxman AD, Wolf F, Davis DA, Herrin J (2006) Continuing education meetings and workshops: Effects on professional practice and health outcomes. *Cochrane Database of Systematic Reviews* **28**(6): 497–526

Victorian Government Department of Human Services (2005) *Competency standards for health and allied health professionals in Australia.* Melbourne: DHS. Available from: http://www.health.vic.gov.au/workforce/downloads/core_clinical_skills_mapping.pdf [Accessed 22 October 2008]

Chapter 15

Stakeholder perspectives on CPD

Introduction

Eve Hutton and Ann Moore

This chapter presents the findings from a study that explored the views of a sample of allied health professionals, health service managers, representatives of professional associations and higher education providers. The study was conducted just prior to the setting up of the Health Professions Council (HPC), established in 2000, and was supported by the then Kent and Sussex education consortia, with the aim of exploring the continuing professional development (CPD) needs of a group of professions known then as the professions allied to medicine (PAMs).

Reviewing the study for this new edition the authors acknowledge that the organisational context may have altered but anticipate that readers will still recognise in the comments made by interviewees, many issues still facing practitioners and other stakeholders today. The authors hope that the recommendations made remain as relevant today as when the study was first published.

Education and training are to be found at the heart of the Department of Health's strategy for allied health professionals (AHPs) (Department of Health, 2008a, 2008b). The HPC requires AHPs to remain competent and up to date through CPD activities and monitors compliance through regular audit (Health Professions Council 2006). Local stakeholders responsible for CPD therefore need to consider how best they can meet the demand for cost-effective CPD initiatives.

Method

The project ran from April 1999–July 2000 (Pringle, 1999, 2000). A qualitative approach was adopted in order to explore the attitudes and perceptions of the key CPD stakeholders and to examine how organisational processes and structures (e.g. appraisal), designed to support CPD within the NHS, work in practice. Case studies were conducted in two joint acute and community NHS trusts within the Kent and Sussex education consortia boundaries. Within the trusts, seven in-depth interviews were carried out with a sample of general managers with responsibility for CPD. Thirteen in-depth interviews were conducted with professional heads of department from occupational therapy, physiotherapy, chiropody, radiography, speech and language therapy, dietetics and clinical psychology.

Eleven focus groups were arranged in the two sites: 63 practitioners from the separate professional groups participated in the focus groups. Contact was made with representatives from the professional associations, and a national network of interested managers, educators and practitioners was established following the publication of a letter in the relevant professional journals, which invited interest in the project. The focus group and individual interview tapes were transcribed verbatim. The analysis used an iterative approach, i.e. transcripts were read repeatedly in order to identify common themes (Glaser and Strauss, 1967; Morgan, 1993). The key themes, outlined below, form the basis for the development of a framework.

Appraisal

Appraisal of NHS staff had become more widespread following the introduction of quality standards into the service (Service First Unit, 1999). Over half of the practitioners in the focus groups had been appraised, in line with the Government's requirement that appraisal systems should be established for all professional staff in the NHS by April 2000 (Department of Health, 1999). Unfilled senior posts were cited as being responsible for the absence of appraisal in some departments, resulting in interruption of the 'cascading down' process. In other cases, reorganisation was given as the reason why appraisal systems had not been put in place:

> We were supposed to introduce appraisal, but there were a thousand other things to do. Do we move services to a new site or do we introduce appraisal? Well it's a fairly obvious answer.
>
> (Radiography manager)

The case study site in which a merger had recently occurred provided an example of how education and training were often the first 'casualty' of reorganisation (Devlin, 1999). Both practitioners and managers were critical of the appraisal system introduced as a part of 'Investors in people', the national standard relating employee development to organisational goals and performance. They described the system as unnecessarily bureaucratic. The quality of appraisal appeared to vary considerably, with some practitioners recounting that it amounted to little more than a 'chat'. For others, it was a more structured and positive experience:

> *It made me stop and think about what I had achieved, what I had been doing and where I might want to go.*
>
> (Practitioner focus group)

Ideally, appraisal should involve preparation from both the manager and the individual before a formal meeting (Mayo, 1998). Comments made during the focus groups suggested that practitioners did not prepare formally for appraisal, seeing this as the line manager's responsibility. Tools already existed that could have helped practitioners make more use of appraisal, such as the use of critical incidents surveys, risk assessment, patient complaints and reflective diaries (Grant and Stanton, 1998). However, there was little evidence that these were either widely understood or used in practice. Practitioners, particularly those trained some time ago, appeared to need support in how to approach CPD, and guidance in the use of needs assessment techniques. Several of the professional managers suggested that they too would have valued more guidance and support concerning their role in appraisal. They felt that their own training needs were often overlooked:

> *So long as I do my job of running the service, people [senior management] are actually very complacent.*
>
> (Occupational therapy manager)

The findings suggested that there needed to be greater appreciation by all stakeholders of the importance of appraisal. The roles and responsibilities of all those involved needed to be clarified at an organisational level in an attempt to make it a genuine starting point for CPD rather than a bureaucratic exercise, carried out to keep the 'Investors in people' sign outside the building.

Portfolios

Fifty-nine percent (*n* = 63) of those participating in the focus groups said that they owned a professional log or portfolio. However, few practitioners were actually using their portfolios as an aid to 'reflective' practice (Schön, 1987). Reasons given were that portfolios were poorly designed, there was insufficient time and that little guidance had been provided to assist practitioners in 'getting started' with them:

> *I was just handed one and said, 'there you go' — I hadn't even been talked through it.*
>
> (Practitioner focus group)

Practitioners who had been working for many years found the task of starting a portfolio daunting. There were many other unresolved issues surrounding portfolios, which emerged during discussions in the focus groups. For example:

- What was the portfolio's role within appraisal?
- If portfolios are to be used in appraisal, should practitioners be allocated work time to complete them?
- To what extent can portfolios fulfil their role as personal documents if they are scrutinised by managers?

Portfolios were likely to become a key component in any mandatory system of CPD, providing a cost-effective, convenient and individual record of learning, based on reflective practice.

There was a lack of clear consensus regarding the role of portfolios within appraisal, and there needed to be discussion leading to the development of clear guidelines. Higher education had a responsibility to ensure that newly qualified practitioners understood the role of portfolios, and that they were equipped with the skills to maintain them on entering practice.

A comment from a manager suggested that this was not always the case:

> *The juniors coming out of college appear to be viewing their portfolios as a folder that they put their certificate of attendance in.*
>
> (Occupational therapy manager)

Higher education could also provide post-registration guidance for practitioners and managers on developing the skills necessary to use portfolios as an effective form of CPD. Those responsible within higher education for delivering a CPD programme, although willing to collaborate, felt that they were constrained by limited resources, particularly lack of time, and the skills necessary to deliver tailor-made, work-based programmes.

Work-based opportunities

There was an imbalance between the provision of opportunities for work-based CPD, compared with external courses in the case-study sites. Attending external courses and conferences was the main source of CPD for most practitioners and managers.

The literature suggested that work-based learning was both effective and cost-effective (Grant and Stanton, 1998). Despite this, work-based education tended to be viewed as limited to the 'latest computer course'. Practitioners whose personal circumstances made it difficult for them to attend courses away from home were keen for more work-based opportunities to be developed. This begged the question as to why work-based opportunities, including portfolio workshops, mentoring and peer supervisory structures and initiatives, such as journal clubs, were not more in evidence. A possible explanation was the way in which training projections and budget allocations were made within the trusts, which created an incentive for managers to use budgets for 'away training'. Managers were often in the position of having to spend money quickly or face losing it, and this did not support longer-term or innovative planning. Managers and practitioners were also in the habit of thinking about education and training in terms of external courses, and the pressure on managers meant that there was little opportunity for them to be creative:

You are in a situation where people are just surviving. You can only really plan CPD when you are confident and you can see a way ahead.

(Speech and language therapy manager)

Higher education providers expressed an interest in developing work-based learning in collaboration with service providers, and there were a few examples where this had taken place. However, they acknowledged that more could have been achieved, specially with regard to the accreditation of work-based learning. One participant felt that at present there was a lot of rhetoric surrounding 'partnerships' between higher education and service providers and that, in reality:

...some managers just want to send their staff on courses and for them to come back ready for work.

(Higher education focus group)

Shared learning

The Government of the time was committed to promoting shared learning, possibly because there was an assumption that it would assist in breaking down 'barriers' between the professions (Hopkins *et al*, 1996). The findings from the project suggested that there needed to be some caution exercised concerning the balance between uniprofessional and shared learning. The case studies highlighted that practitioners were working in increasingly specialist areas, and their CPD needs were often linked directly to their specialism. Practitioners felt that shared learning, at a post-registration level, should complement not replace specialist professional education and training. Few shared initiatives for CPD existed, suggesting that there was room for development in this area. One possible reason for the lack of shared initiatives could have been the fact that PAMs forums in trusts were difficult to establish. Problems of communication between the separate professions, struggles over how they represented one another at board level and the challenge of maintaining continuity in an ever-changing NHS limited their effectiveness. As a consequence, PAMs were limited in their ability to collaborate with one another and in their ability to influence decision-making at a strategic level:

We did have a forum where we met as PAMs, but it seems to have gone by the wayside. It was supposed to have been our link with the board.
(Occupational therapy manager)

Local shared learning initiatives may have been more likely to emerge if these forums for PAMs had become established and if the separate professions had recognised their joint agenda, adopting a 'strength in numbers' approach to lobbying for resources and funding. Bringing about a culture change that would support both shared and work-based CPD presented a challenge. If shared learning and work-based CPD initiatives were to be successfully integrated at a practice level, similar strategies to those used to promote evidence-based practice, aimed at changing attitudes, needed to be considered (Dunning *et al*, 1998). Managers crucially needed to be allowed the time to develop longer-term strategic plans for training and development. Additionally, they needed to be offered practical assistance, in the form of a CPD facilitator, in how to approach the task of developing accredited work-based and shared opportunities for practitioners. Funding and budgetary arrangements within trusts would have needed to be more creatively allocated in order to provide incentives for managers to develop such initiatives.

Evaluating CPD and making use of 'new' knowledge and skills

Both the trusts involved in the project had attempted to put in place CPD evaluation systems. However, these focused on the quantifiable aspects of time and costs associated with CPD, and an assessment of the impact on practitioner's effectiveness or benefits to patient care had not been attempted:

> *The actual evaluation was very general....it amounted to how many training days we had related to how much we spent, and it did sound good and cheap.*
>
> (Occupational therapy manager)

The literature indicated that the successful integration of new knowledge depended on it being reinforced in the clinical setting (Grant and Stanton, 1998). The findings from the study, however, suggested that many practitioners felt that there was little opportunity for them to apply new skill and ability:

> *It's a waste of time if we spend time learning something and then don't use it to its full potential.*
>
> (Radiography focus group)

This appeared to be a specific problem for practitioners who had worked towards a higher degree. Many of them were frustrated by the fact that although they gained personal satisfaction, their work had not changed to accommodate their new skills. A few of the managers interviewed simply did not see an MSc as a useful form of CPD. One radiography manager stated that there was little point in sending a practitioner on an MSc course because 'it was of no value to the trust' and of little value to the individual because 'we are not going to promote them'.

From a general management perspective, however, the frustration that some practitioners experienced was the result of the failure to match professional needs to the wider business plan of the trust. Few practitioners were familiar with the business plan, describing it as a 'public relations exercise'. Professional managers influenced the way in which practitioners perceived the organisation in which they worked, and it appeared that it was down to the skills of the individual professional manager to translate the business plan into meaningful, tangible learning goals for practitioners.

Communication and collaboration between stakeholders

Barriers in communication and collaboration between the separate professions can be explained partly as emanating from the era of inter- and intra-trust competition pursued by the Conservative Government in the 1980s (Department of Health, 1989). There was little evidence of the new spirit of partnership and collaboration, despite rhetoric to this effect (Department of Health, 1998). The separate professions found it difficult to grasp the opportunities of 'working together' for a shared aim, possibly because they lacked the necessary skills (Alter and Jerald, 1993). A lack of understanding among stakeholders about the education consortia contributed to confusion about their role in CPD. Each trust was responsible for developing CPD initiatives under the requirements of clinical governance, but the commitment to creating an overall strategic vision at the level of the consortia had not been grasped. Higher education representatives felt that the consortia could assume more of a coordinating role:

It would have been sensible if there could be one person who could be responsible for channelling the CPD needs [of the consortia] through us.
(Higher education provider)

Some participants argued that PAMs had been thrown together organisationally simply because they were not nurses or doctors. Others indicated that PAMs were beginning to develop a shared agenda. The strategic planning of CPD among PAMs and between separate provider units was an, as yet, uncharted area offering enormous potential for the future commissioning of higher education. The publication of the Department of Health's strategy (Department of Health, 2000a) may have acted to stimulate such developments. Establishing a policy on CPD within the confederation would have had an immediate benefit in assisting higher education providers in developing courses or facilitator-based workplace initiatives that meet the needs of several provider units.

Conclusions

What clearly emerges from analysis of the data is the need to ensure that the foundations necessary for CPD are in place. Practitioners working in departments that are inadequately staffed will not prioritise CPD. Similarly, if appraisal systems are poor, CPD needs will not be identified. Therefore, practitioners need to be supported by adequate workforce planning, a professional manager skilled in staff development and an effective appraisal scheme.

A recent study carried out in the south west region of England found that similar issues to those identified continue to present a challenge to AHPs' access to and participation in CPD (Gibbs, 2011). Gibbs highlights significant areas that continue to require improvement including communication between higher education institutions and clinical staff, the need for more work-based opportunities for learning and the need to facilitate the integration of new knowledge into practice through reflection. This project demonstrated the importance of approaching CPD from a joint stakeholder perspective. Widespread enthusiasm and support for CPD exists, but in order to harness this, the professions and other key stakeholders need to collaborate, particularly when financial pressures on the NHS increase and the need to deliver cost-effective solutions to CPD become more pressing.

Key points

The Kent and Sussex education consortia project for post-registration education of PAMs and clinical psychology identified the following areas of priorities:

• In order for practitioners to engage in CPD, they need to be supported by adequate workforce planning, a professional manager skilled in staff development and an effective appraisal scheme
• More work-based and shared learning opportunities in CPD need to be established for AHPs
• Representation of AHPs and clinical psychologists at a senior level within trusts is necessary in order to highlight the specific CPD needs of these professions
• Closer collaboration needs to occur between the separate professions and the separate stakeholders in developing a shared CPD agenda

Acknowledgements
The authors would like to acknowledge the support of both the Kent and Sussex education consortia. Grateful thanks to all those individuals who participated in and contributed to professions allied to medicine post-registration education project.

References

Alter C, Jerald H (1993) *Organizations working together.* Sage, London

Department of Health (1989) *Working for patients* HMSO: London

Department of Health (1998) *The new NHS: Modern, dependable.* HMSO: London

Department of Health (1999) *Continuing professional development: Quality in the new NHS.* HMSO: London.

Department of Health (2005) *A national framework to support local workforce strategy development.* HMSO, London

Department of Health (2000a) *Modernising regulation – The new Health Professions Council.* Department of Health, London: 13

Department of Health (2000b) *A health Service of all the talents: Developing the NHS workforce. A consultation document on the review of workforce planning.* HMSO, London

Department of Health (2008a) *Framing the contribution of allied health professionals: delivering high quality care.* HMSO, London

Department of Health (2008b) *Modernising allied health professions (AHP) careers: A competency based career framework.* HMSO, London

Devlin M (1999) States of flux. *Health Service Journal* **6 May:** 24–5

Dunning M, Abi-Aad G, Gilbert D, Gillam S, Livett H (1998) *Turning evidence into everyday practice.* Falmer Press, London

Gibbs V (2011) An investigation into the challenges facing the future provision of continuing professional development for allied health professionals in a changing healthcare environment. *Radiography* **17**(2): 152–7

Grant J, Stanton F (1998) *The effectiveness of continuing professional development — A report for the Chief Medical Officer's review of CPD in practice.* Joint Centre for Education in Medicine, London

Glaser B, Strauss A (1967) *The discovery of grounded theory.* Aldine Publishing, Chicago

Health Professions Council (2006) Y*our guide to our standards for continuing professional development.* Available from: www.hpc-uk.org.

Hopkins A, Solomon J, Abelson J (1996) Shifting boundaries in professional care. *Journal of the Royal Society of Medicine* **89**(7): 364–71

Mayo A (1998) *Developing a training and development strategy.* Institute of Personnel and Development, London

Morgan D (1993) *Successful focus groups: Advancing the state of the art.* Sage, London

Pringle E (1999) Post-registration education: Exploring the issues for PAMs. *British Journal of Therapy and Rehabilitation* **6**(12): 591–4

Pringle E (2000) *Pushing an open door — A stakeholder approach to developing CPD initiatives for PAMs and clinical psychology.* Research Centre for Health Professions, University of Brighton, Brighton

Service First Unit (1999) *A guide to quality schemes for the public sector.* Cabinet Office, London

Schön D (1987) *Educating the reflective practitioner: Towards a new design for teaching and learning in the professions.* Josey Bass, San Francisco

Chapter 16

The HPC audit: a personal perspective

Introduction

Deborah Harrison, Jennie Vitkovitch and Jo Geere

This chapter is written by an occupational therapist (OT), a physiotherapist (PT) and a speech and language therapist (SLT) from their personal perspective of having been selected for audit by the Health Professions Council (HPC) and successfully submitting the required profile and documents. It also describes a particular point of view, that of established practitioners who were not originally educated to document their continued professional development (CPD). New graduates to the profession will be engaged in these processes as second nature and they will have been guided from the first day of their degree course to have an organised approach to their CPD and keeping a record of it. Those of us who have been around for a while have engaged with all sorts of interesting CPD but have perhaps resisted the idea of writing it all down and keeping records. We have known for some years that we are required to keep a portfolio and felt pleased if we put a few attendance certificates in a lever arch file. Over time, however, the broader ideas about what constitutes CPD and the value of writing as part of the reflective process filtered through our consciousness. Nevertheless, when the letter arrived from the HPC stating, 'you have been selected for audit', the feeling was generally of shock and slight panic.

Where do you start? The HPC sends a booklet with the letter and there is useful information on its website. In summary the healthcare practitioner selected for audit has to submit a CPD profile consisting of a job summary of 500 words and a statement of CPD activities over the past two years in 1500 words. The statement has to be supported with evidence from the practitioner's records.

This chapter is not a substitute for looking at the guidance offered by the HPC, but is written with the aim of sharing the personal experience and giving some ideas how to go about the task.

Job summary

The first step to writing a job summary is to find your job description and outline the bare bones of what you do from that. Then you can expand. Within the job description there might be sub-headings that you can use to organise the description. Clinicians might have administrative, management and clinical aspects to their role. Educators will have teaching, administration and research or scholarship aspects to their job. This breaks down the writing into smaller chunks and makes the description more organised. There is an example in *Box 16.1* from an occupational therapist who is an educator in higher education.

Personal statement

The personal statement is the more daunting of the profile documents to write. It needs to demonstrate that you have not only been engaged in CPD, but also have recorded it and have met the five standards of practice. The first step is to draw together what you have. This might be filed neatly in one place, but it might not. You could, for example, have paper documents in a file and electronic documents on your computer. If you have an annual appraisal or review process this is a good place to start because these documents will record what you have achieved and your ongoing plans, hopefully linking your personal objectives with those of the organisation that you work in. You can build on this outline to expand and add in evidence. Once you have gathered all your documents together you can start to write the personal statement. One way to organise this is to address each standard in turn, using sub-headings, and this also makes it explicit how you have met the requirements. Within each standard the narrative must also connect with the job description.

Standard I

Registrants must maintain a continuous and up-to-date record of their CPD activities.

The HPC in their guide to completing the profile gives a main question to be answered and supplementary questions. The main question asks if your evidence includes a summary sheet of CPD activities. As you have to submit this document as the first piece of evidence, this question will automatically be addressed.

Box 16.1. Summary of recent work/practice

I am employed as a lecturer in a health school in a University. My work roles can be divided into three areas: teaching, administration and research or scholarly activity. These three areas will be described in turn.

Teaching: I teach mainly on pre-registration programmes in occupational therapy and physiotherapy at both BSc and MSc level. I also teach a small amount to speech and language therapy BSc students. I develop and deliver teaching in the following subjects: psychology and health psychology within the BSc and MSc human sciences modules for occupational therapy and physiotherapy, mental health practice in the BSc and MSc occupational therapy modules, and qualitative research methods in the BSc occupational therapy, physiotherapy and speech and language therapy programmes. I supervise BSc and MSc research dissertations. In the next academic year I will teach on an interprofessional MSc in mental health. I also deliver post-registration short courses for clinicians.

I am an academic advisor for occupational therapy students on the BSc and MSc programmes. I visit practice placements in a variety of health and social care settings around the region throughout the academic year. I undertake the marking of a range of assignments within the BSc and MSc programmes.

Administration: I have recently been appointed as Director of Teaching and Learning for the school which is a key role in terms of assuring the quality of the teaching and student experience. I work closely with course directors and senior administrators to fulfil my responsibilities. I will attend staff and student liaison committees to ensure that I have a link with the student body. I am a member of the school executive group and will contribute to the general management of the school.

I am also a module co-ordinator for two research modules in the MSc occupational therapy and physiotherapy programmes. This involves co-ordinating the teaching and assessment, assuring appropriate content, maintaining a high quality programme, and collecting and responding to student feedback.

Research and scholarly activity: My research is focused on mental health and social inclusion. I am developing a research project within the context of my PhD which will explore the experiences of people with mental health difficulties when they engage with mainstream education. I am also working with a group of people who have used mental health services to develop collaborative research to ensure that research is done with people and not to them. We are currently working on including the stories of people with mental health issues in a mainstream living history archive. My research feeds directly into my teaching at pre- and post-registration level.

You then need to state that you have kept an up-to-date and accurate record. Accuracy should not be an issue, assuming that healthcare professionals are honest, but many find it a challenge to attend to their portfolio on a very regular basis. Therefore, answer this by saying exactly what you have got and how you usually collect the evidence. Finally, the registrant should state whether anyone has approved a plan of CPD activities and this is where appraisal or supervision documents will prove helpful.

The records that you keep may take many forms and they might not necessarily be in one folder sitting on a shelf, neatly labelled 'portfolio'. *Chapter 1* in this book discusses this in more detail. The key point to bear in mind is that this is a personal record and will accumulate over many years. One file will not be enough and may not capture your learning and development in a way that is meaningful for you. Two examples are given in *Box 16.2* that describe how the

---

Box 16.2. Standard 1

Example 1

I have maintained a continuous, up-to-date and accurate record of my CPD activities. I have two sets of documents that record these activities. One relates to my work role and the key documents included in that file are those related to my annual appraisal. This includes self-appraisals, plans for the forthcoming year and feedback from the Head of School. It also includes reflective records. These documents will be referred to in the following sections. The second set of documents records my learning as a post-graduate student and this was commenced in September 2008. The activities recorded here are closely linked with learning for my work role, but they are kept separate for ease of reference. This record includes annual review, supervision records and significant learning events. My first piece of evidence is a summary list of CPD activities undertaken over the past two years, which is drawn from these two sets of documents.

Example 2

I have kept a CPD portfolio over the past 2 years which I update as I regularly complete professional development activities. This is comprised of a folder in which I keep paper copies of relevant documents such as attendance certificates and course programmes, as well as electronic folders storing documentation of my CPD activities.

---

registrants, one an OT (Example 1) and one a PT (Example 2) recorded their learning in the two years leading up to the audit.

The Royal College of Speech and Language Therapists (RCSLT) has provided its members with a number of useful CPD tools over the past five years, including a CPD Newsletter and a 'toolkit'. Most importantly, SLTs have had access, through the RCSLT, to an online diary facility since April 2005. This is an invaluable way of recording all CPD activities and provides an easily accessible format in which to review activities carried out. Entries are categorised according to the HPC descriptors of CPD activity. In addition you record the number of hours on each activity, your learning, and any other comments. There is a facility to relate the activities to the Knowledge and Skills Framework (KSF). So, when selected for audit, SLTs are able to download their diary for the required period of time and use it as evidence of fulfilling Standard 1; this really makes the audit process much easier for individuals to manage. The diary entries can easily be scanned in order to find activities and associated learning to submit as evidence for the remaining Standards.

Standard 2

Registrants must demonstrate that their CPD activities are a mixture of learning activities relevant to current or future practice.

The main questions posed by the HPC not only ask you about the different types of activity undertaken, but also ask you to make a connection with the relevance to your work role. It might be useful to divide this part of the statement into sections with sub-headings relating to the 500-word summary of job role, for example the three headings previously suggested; administration, management and clinical (see Job summary above). The relevance will then be obvious.

When considering the type of CPD activities undertaken and demonstrating a mixture, it will help to look at the HPC website where it lists a wide variety of activities that count as learning, education and development. Most registered practitioners will know that CPD is so much more than attending courses, but it is worth repeating that fact again here. Every day will present new people to encounter and the ever-changing context of health and social care delivery presents new challenges. The chapters of this book give many examples of CPD and how to record it. *Box 16.3* gives two examples of the types of activities identified by registrants in their statement, one an OT (Example 1) and one a PT (Example 2).

Box 16.3. Standard 2

Example 1

Evidence document number 1 demonstrates that my CPD involves a mixture of learning activities relevant to my current or future practice. Much of my CPD takes place as 'reflection on action' as I respond to changing roles and responsibilities. These are recorded as critical incidents or more formally in the annual appraisal process. The annual appraisal is also important to determine future work roles and development needs. I have also attended formal training and education events. The evidence for these might be given in written work or presentations, formal assignments and reflective tools, like significant learning events.

Example 2

My CPD activities are varied and reflect the diversity of roles which my post as a physiotherapist encompasses. They include; formal learning, work-based learning, student feedback, peer review, self-directed learning and professional activities. Appropriate CPD activities which link to my work roles are identified and planned through a process of reflection, discussion of my professional development plan with a professional and academic mentor and confirmation of the plan by my mentor and the head of service. In this way I ensure that planned CPD will link to and build on previous activities to ensure progressive professional development which is closely linked to my work roles.

Standard 3

Registrants must seek to ensure that their CPD has contributed to the quality of their practice.

In the HPC guidance for completing the CPD profile, Standards 3 and 4 are addressed together. It makes sense to address ensuring the quality of the service and benefiting the service user together in one section because the narrative can flow better and make direct links. It might make more sense for some practitioners, however, to separate out these two standards. If someone is working in education or management it might help to consider quality before defining who the service users are and how they benefit. *Box 16.4* gives an example from someone working in education. These two sections are the most important part of the profile and should be the main focus of the statement.

Box 16.4. Standard 3

Administration: My new management role has a particular emphasis on maintaining and improving the quality of teaching and learning. I am looking forward to working across the school and linking with the wider faculty and university. In the modules that I currently co-ordinate and teach on, I am always looking for ways to improve the currency of the teaching and to respond to student feedback. Evidence document 7 is my self-appraisal from the academic year 2008-09 and provides examples of the actions taken to improve the quality of the teaching that my colleagues and I provide.

Standard 4

Registrants must seek to ensure that their CPD benefits the service user.

For many registrants the identity of the service user will be obvious, it will be the patients or clients receiving therapy services. This will not be the case for everyone. It might be useful to define who the direct service user is, for example the team of staff that you manage or the students that you teach. Then the connection between your work and the service directly offered to service users can be discussed. *Box 16.5* gives two examples, again, one from an OT (Example 1) and one from a PT (Example 2).

Standard 5

You must fill in and return a CPD profile, and evidence of your CPD, when we ask you to.

This standard will be met when you place the envelope in the post, on time, containing the profile and the evidence.

The evidence

The HPC makes it clear that it does not want registrants to send everything that they have. It is necessary to select and edit the records that you have kept. The

---

Box 16.5. Standard 4

Example 1

As an occupational therapist teaching in a university I feel that it still remains a priority for my work to benefit people who use health and social care services, even though I do not have direct contact with patients or clients now. The more obvious service users in my present role are: students, academic colleagues and clinical partners.

Example 2

I have continuously updated my professional practice, knowledge and skills through regular self-directed and collaborative review of research literature directly relevant to my own teaching content and research activities, organisation of and attendance at professional post-graduate short courses and conferences as well as regularly collecting feedback from peer review of all aspects of my work. Combined with my own reflection on my performance and practice, I actively implement changes to my work.

---

decision about what to select will be based on what you need to back up what you have described in your statement. Even if you make a reflective diary entry every Friday afternoon, you only need to send one to illustrate that this is a part of your personal CPD. You may not need to send a complete document if it is very lengthy, an edited version can give an example more effectively. A variety of small examples will be more illustrative of achieving the standards than pages and pages of reflection. *Box 16.6* provides an example from an occupational therapist and one from a speech and language therapist.

Final thoughts and reflections

Being selected for audit by the HPC is a significant event and brings up many thoughts and feelings. It is scary because, although the majority of registered practitioners are committed to their own development and to providing a high quality service, there is always that doubt that perhaps you have not done enough or have not done the correct things. Some personal reflections follow which demonstrate a variety of reactions. These reflections do not include the reactions of practitioners who were selected and could not produce the evidence or

Box 16.6. Evidence		
Evidence no. and brief description	No. of pages or description of evidence format	CPD standard that evidence relates to
Occupational therapist		
1 A list of CPD activities undertaken in the last two years	4 pages of a table listing CPD activities	Standard 1
2 Reflections on an incident related to student support.	1 page critical incident form	Standard 2
3 Edited version of management review	1 page	Standard 2
4 Personal statement submitted for course application	1 page	Standard 2
5 Significant learning event arising from research methods course	SLE form 1 page	Standard 2
6 Write up of psychology review meeting	Meeting minutes	Standard 3
7 Extract from self-appraisal document	1 page	Standard 3
8 Programme for short course delivered to mental health OTs	1 page	Standard 4
Speech and language therapist		
1 RCSLT Online diary record May 2007 to August 2009	12 pages	Standards 1, 2
2 MAHEP module 1: Introduction and feedback summary	5 pages	Standards 3, 4
3 MAHEP module 3: proposal and feedback summary	3 pages	Standards 3, 4
4 PDP documents 2007-8 and 2008-9/10	6 pages	Standards 3, 4
5. Student feedback summaries on teaching 2007–8 & 2008–9	6 pages	Standard 4
		Box 16.6 cont/

Box 16.6. cont/		
6 Attendance at ICAN course: Speech, Language & Communication Needs in Secondary Age Children	1 page	Standard 3
7 Short Course Power Point presentation Summary of Evaluation form and comments	3 pages	Standards 3, 4
8 Assignment feedback sheets from Masters Module: Introduction to research methods	6 pages	Standards 3, 4

submitted unsuccessfully; fortunately, this has not been our experience. Overall, although time-consuming and somewhat anxiety-provoking, it has been an interesting experience that affirms our commitment to our work and profession. The final piece of advice would be: keep up to date with your portfolio and be prepared; it could be your turn next.

Personal reflections

Example 1

I felt pretty confident that I would not be selected for audit in the first round of occupational therapists to be considered. There are lots of us and the chances of being one of the first were slim, or so I thought. Anyway, I had been engaged in CPD activities and had records (albeit in a variety of places and formats), so why worry? When I received the letter, however, I wasn't quite so calm and immediately set about pulling everything together. I discovered that I was far better organised than I thought and had achieved quite a lot over the past two years.

When the personal statement was written and the evidence selected, it felt quite affirming. Then I had to wait. In my anxiety to get the job done, I sent it off way before the submission date and it seemed to take ages to get a response from the HPC. Then a letter arrived and I felt stupidly anxious about the contents. It was just confirming, however, that they had received my stuff and it would be a further six weeks. Finally a short letter came through saying, in two lines, that my submission had been accepted. I felt relieved that after nearly 30 years as an occupational therapist, I could carry on. I also felt a little flat and in a childish way wanted someone to give some evaluation of what I'd sent, or just a pat on the back and well done. An unreasonable thought I know, but it was how I felt at the time.

Example 2

I must admit that my heart sank when I received the letter from the HPC informing me that I had been selected for audit; it was a lovely sunny day and I was sitting outside in the garden with a cup of tea, having just got home from work. I wondered if I would be able to fulfil their requirements, and the thought of not being able to do so was almost paralysing. However, having read the *How to complete your CPD profile* booklet sent by HPC I took a deep breath and turned to my online diary to seek out the appropriate evidence.

I was glad that I had been fairly strict about keeping my diary up to date; it is quite easy to let this slip in the press of other demands on our time. The most demanding activity was constructing the CPD profile (job summary and personal statement), but the HPC sample profiles were very useful guides, as were statements I had supporting job applications, CVs, etc. The guidance booklet was an invaluable resource in explaining the process to go through and answered all my questions. One of the most difficult decisions to make was concerning how much evidence to submit; I worried whether it would it be too much or too little. Again I referred to the guidance booklet and the sample profile to steer me in the right direction. The letter informing me I had been selected for audit arrived early in July; the evidence needed to be submitted by the end of September. By mid-August I decided I needed to complete the process as it was beginning to feel a bit daunting, so I set aside a day to do this. I was glad I did so. Gathering the evidence, printing it off, putting it in an envelope and sending it off to the HPC immediately triggered a feeling of relief which was probably equalled on the day I received the letter informing me that my audit had been approved!

Yes, it was a scary process, but having been through it once I will not be so worried when next selected, and it gave me an opportunity to reflect in a considered way on just how much and what type of CPD activities I had engaged in over the previous 2 years.

Key points

- Being selected for the HPC audit can be daunting
- The HPC provides clear guidance on what documentation needs to be submitted
- The personal statement and supporting evidence must meet the five standards of practice
- The HPC audit can be a valuable opportunity to reflect on the previous two years of CPD

Index